KILLING MAGELLAN
in the Philippine Gold Islands

THE UNTOLD CONSPIRACY and BEYOND

By

Myrna J. de la Paz

[signature: Myrna J. de la Paz]

[handwritten: myrnamulhern @ g.mail.com]

"The one duty we owe to history is to rewrite it."
-Oscar Wilde

PUBLISHED BY GOLDPHIN MEDIA LLC

Los Angeles, California

Registered With the Writers Guild of America, 2018

Copyright 2019, Library of Congress

Washington DC

DEDICATED TO

THE PEOPLE OF THE PHILIPPINES

"History is always written by the winners. When Two cultures clash,
the loser is obliterated, and the winner writes the history books -
books which glorify their own cause and disparage the conquered
foe." - Dan Brown, the Da Vinci Code

CONTENTS

CHAPTER V. MAGELLAN in BAUG ISLAND,
MAZZAUA

Magellan's Show of Force and Firepower: a Threat. Pigafetta on Rajah Si Ayo's Balangay Boat. Natives' Use of Porcelain Jars and Dishes. Pigafetta at the Royal Hunting Lodge. Rajah Kalambu, the King of Butuan-Kalagan. The Golden Palace of Rajah Kalambu. The Royal Hunting Ground.

CHAPTER VI. THE FIRST MASS on PHILIPPINE SOIL

Planting Christianity in the Land of Abba. The Mass in Baug, Mazzaua. Discovery of Mindanao Gold: The Real Significance of the First Mass. Staking the Spanish Claim with the Cross. Magellan Starts Move to Conquer the Gold Islands.

CHAPTER VII. THE BEGINNING of the
NATIVE CONSPIRACY

Rajah Si Ayo Changes His Mind. Delaying Tactics of the Two Kings. Magellan Maintains Disguised Stance Regarding Gold. The Rajahnate of Mazzaua. The Natives of the Rice Farming Village in Baug, Mazzaua. The Natural Resources of Mazzaua. Mazzaua in Old Maps. The Butuan Rajahnate. Butuan-Kalagan: Ancient Country in the pre-Philippine Islands. The Butuan-Kalagan Gold Country. The People of Butuan-Kalagan.

The Sama People in Butuan-Kalagan. The Sama-Manobo-Bisaya Expansion and Influence. Magellan Sails to Cebu with Rajah Si Ayo. Rajah Si Ayo's Additional Delaying Tactics.

CHAPTER VIII. MAGELLAN ARRIVES in CEBU
The Rajahnate of Cebu. The Socio-Political Structure of the Cebu Rajahnate. Magellan's Aggressive Arrival in Cebu. Meeting Rajah Humabon (Umabong), King of Cebu. The Role of the Rajah of Mazzaua in the Cebu Conspiracy. Magellan Delivers More Threats. Magellan Becomes an Evangelist. Magellan Prescribes Obedience and Chastity. Rajah Humabon: Description. Prince Tupas.
Magellan's Gold Policy in Cebu. The People of Cebu and Their Homes.

CHAPTER IX. MAGELLAN SETS FOOT
on SUGBO SOIL
Drama on Baptism Day. Magellan Delivers Death Threats. Setting Up of the Cross and the Burning of Idols. The Burning of Bullaia (Buaya). The Issue of Unburned Indigenous Idols. The Healing Miracle of the Sick Man: a Scapegoat. Reckoning with the Renegade.

KILLING MAGELLAN
in the Philippine Gold Islands

THE UNTOLD CONSPIRACY and BEYOND

By

Myrna J. de la Paz

INTRODUCTION

The Untold Native Resistance and Conspiracy

Killing Magellan presents the story of the first successful united but untold indigenous conspiracy and resistance in the pre-Philippines against Spanish conquest during the 16th century European Age of Discovery. The conspiracy shattered Ferdinand Magellan's ambitious, bold, and reckless attempt to conquer the pre-Philippine gold islands. The native conspiracy resulted in Magellan's voyage in the pre-Philippines becoming a debacle, and Magellan's untimely death in Mactan, a small island in the kingdom of Cebu.

The book also reveals Magellan's secret personal agenda behind his daring, death-defying voyage on a westward route bound for the Moluccas (Spice Islands) in Southeast Asia. Shortly after his arrival in the pre-Philippines, his hidden motive drove Magellan to initiate a game of deception that the natives on their part were compelled to play in defense of their homeland.

Along with the uncovering of the native conspiracy, and Magellan's hidden agenda, my investigation has also brought up the noteworthy but disregarded participation of Enrique, Magellan's slave. Enrique's importance and value hold strong connections to Magellan's secret but compelling reasons for taking a voyage no one before him had ever dared to take. When the voyage reached the pre-Philippines, Magellan used Enrique as his interpreter.

1

Enrique spoke Cebuano, a Vijaya/Vizzaya language widely spoken in the Vijaya cultural region that includes the Vizzaya islands and Mindanao. Scott, an American historian contends that "...the northern and eastern coasts of Mindanao were part of the Visayan culture area: from Surigao in the east to Sindangan Bay in the west, missionaries were able to make themselves understood in Cebuano" (William Henry Scott, Barangay, Ateneo de Manila University Press, (1994), p.161).

Coming back to his homeland might have been the realization of Enrique's dream, but this event took on a much broader significance which Enrique himself may never even have realized. Enrique had achieved a world record. Enrique's homecoming to the pre-Philippines inadvertently made him the first man to circumnavigate the world.

The Myths of Magellan's Voyage in the Pre-Philippines

The whole world knows about Ferdinand Magellan's historic voyage, but what has been written so far in the history books about the arrival of Magellan's expedition, and his death in the Philippines, comes closer to fiction rather than the truth. To this day, biased or misguided accounts replete with intentional or unintentional misrepresentations, misconceptions, distortions, and omissions of facts have created myths that continue to persist in the narrative of Magellan's visit in the 16th century, and his encounter with the indigenous people of the islands.

Originally interpreted by 16th and 17th century Spanish friars and historians, the mainstream versions were written from the point of view of the Spanish colonizers of the Philippines. The myths of Magellan's voyage in the pre-Philippines found in the mainstream history books used in the Philippine school system about pre-Hispanic history and culture in the Philippines are derived from the 1906 English translation of Blair and Robertson.

This itself came from five sources, namely: Antonio Pigafetta's account of Magellan's Voyage (1522), Miguel de Loarca's Relacion (1582), Juan Plasencia's Treatises on Customs, Laws and Religious Practices (1589), Pedro Chirino's Relacion (1604), and Antonio de Morga's Sucsesos (1609) (Scott, 1).

Although the Spaniards might have read and written their own interpretations of Pigafetta's eyewitness account of Magellan's voyage in the pre-Philippines with good intentions, they expressed their ideas within the framework of the colonization efforts and the objectives of the Spanish empire. Undoubtedly, as Spanish colonizers, they looked at Pigafetta's narrative through a lens colored by their cultural prejudices, biases, and colonial political agendas.

The truth about Magellan's voyage in the pre-Philippines lies hidden in the untold story embedded in the sequence of events, between the lines of Pigafetta's narrative, and in the underlying dynamics of the interactions between Magellan and the natives during the last seven weeks of his life.

Pigafetta's relatively independent report reveals many of the missing facts and truths about this world-changing event, but misunderstood piece of world history. A close examination of Pigafetta's account also sheds light on the misinformation and myths regarding the first face-to-face contacts and interactions between Magellan, his navigational crew, and the indigenous Austronesian ancestors of the Filipinos.

Although the myths of Magellan's voyage in the pre-Philippine gold islands have been around for almost five hundred years, it is never too late to find and know the truth. Considering the magnitude of Magellan's historic expedition that forever changed the world, the untold story of Magellan's coming to the pre-Philippines, and the real reasons that led to his untimely death, deserve to be told.

Moreover, the timeless and universal nature of truth validates the rewriting of history, establishing its relevance and potential impact on people's lives today, and in the future, no matter how long ago the events may have happened in the past. Giving truth a chance can also, after all, unleash its liberating and transformative power.

The Mainstream Version

Ferdinand Magellan's voyage has been the stuff of legend, and has inspired travelers, explorers, adventurers, and dreamers all over the world from the 16th century up to the present time. The grandeur of his ambition and his extraordinary courage on a voyage no one before him had ever dared to make have challenged and inspired the imagination of many generations for almost five hundred years. His record in the world of exploration and discovery had been unmatched until the 20th century when in 1969 American astronauts traveled from earth to space, and made the first human landing on the moon.

While much has been written about Magellan's life and adventures for centuries, details of the authentic events and circumstances leading to his death have been limited and obscure. As a result, Magellan's death has been a mystery if not an aberration. It was an untimely end for a man who was within reach of the rewards for which he had risked his life. Magellan's death was anticlimactic, an unexpected tragic conclusion to a story that was supposed to have had a happy if not a great ending.

Magellan never made it back to Spain, the starting point of his voyage. He was killed in the island of Mactan, in the Philippines, just 400 miles from the official destination of the voyage, the fabled spice islands of the Moluccas in Southeast Asia.

The mainstream version of the story of Magellan's voyage in the pre-Philippines has been around since the 17th century, and has found its way to educational institutions and history circles around the world. It has been accepted as historical fact

4

for almost five centuries. The version goes like this: after finding a westward route from Spain to Southeast Asia across the Pacific on his way to the Moluccas, Magellan discovered the islands now known as the Philippines.

In the kingdom of Cebu, the King, his chief men, and hundreds of his people without resistance willingly accepted Magellan's offer to convert to Christianity. They were all baptized, and pledged loyalty to the Spanish King who was also the Emperor of the Holy Roman Empire. Their baptism technically made them subjects of the Emperor. Only Lapu-Lapu, the Chief of Mactan, and his followers refused to be converted. Several weeks later, with his ships, Magellan crossed the narrow channel to Mactan to confront Lapu-Lapu. In the ensuing battle, Magellan was killed.

Except for the fact that Magellan dies at the end, the mainstream story sounds too good to be true. Parts of the story defy the workings of normal human behavior in relation to territorial invasion, and defense. A strange event in the mainstream version is the mass baptism all in one day of 800 natives along with Rajah Humabon (Umabong), the King of Cebu, supposedly a friendly king who saw the superiority of the Christian religion. It has to be noted that the mass baptisms took place just one week after Magellan's sudden and unexpected arrival in the city of Cebu, at that time the largest and richest international port in the southern Philippines, if not the whole Philippine archipelago.

Humabon was a rajah, a paramount ruler who ruled a kingdom with a port engaged in foreign trade (Scott, 220). He was the king of the trade center in the Vijaya cultural region of the Vijaya (Vizzaya) islands and Mindanao, and part of the 16th century international Southeast Asian trading network. Why did Rajah Humabon simply agree without any resistance to put himself, his people, his international port, and his kingdom under the rule of the Spanish Emperor?

Anyone who would care enough to give this scenario some serious thought would know that the mainstream story of the supposed willingness of hundreds of natives to readily agree to the mass baptism is highly improbable to say the least.

5

While the event really did take place, there must be a deeper logic or a more compelling reason for Rajah Humabon to lead his people to agree to get baptized just a week after the surprise arrival of strange white foreigners from the other side of the world in the port city of Sugbo (Cebu), the center of his kingdom.

The second issue is Magellan's defeat and death in Mactan. Considering the power and capacity of the Spanish Empire in war and conquest during the Age of Exploration and Discovery in the 16th century, I find it difficult to comprehend Magellan's defeat and death while trying to subdue just one, stubborn, rebellious chieftain named Lapu-Lapu in the small island of Mactan in the kingdom of Cebu.

Magellan was an experienced, highly-skilled soldier famous for his fighting prowess in several Portuguese wars of conquest before he became the captain of the Spanish expedition to the Moluccas. Moreover, Magellan's fleet had superior fire power. His ships were equipped with cannons, the most destructive weapons of the day. His men had guns, crossbows, metal shields, and metal body armor, and they fought against near-naked natives in loincloths with wicker shields, armed only with bolos (machetes), spears, and bows and arrows. Yet, in spite of Magellan's superior weapons of war, he ended up dead on the shore of the small island of Mactan. Magellan died in a minor encounter. His death does not make sense. How and why did it happen? I figured the answers to my questions were hidden in an untold story.

Thinking like a history detective, I wanted to know how and why Magellan was killed under the most unlikely circumstances. I started my investigation by reading *Magellan's Voyage, a Narrative Account of the First Circumnavigation*, the eyewitness account written by Antonio Pigafetta, the chronicler of the voyage. To my surprise, I uncovered a large part of the untold story of Magellan's voyage and death in the Philippines inside Pigafetta's narrative, the same source used as a reference by the Spanish friars and historians who wrote the first mainstream version.

Gross omissions in the mainstream Spanish version, however, have resulted in a significant departure from Pigafetta's account in a number of ways that covered up the true but untold story of the arrival of Magellan, and his death in the pre-Philippines.

Having uncovered a story kept secret and hidden in the dark pages of world history for nearly five hundred years, I realized the importance and urgency of sharing my discovery with everyone who would consider the wisdom of knowing the truth.

Finding the Untold Story

Finding the untold story of Magellan's arrival and death in the Philippines involved a thorough reading of Pigafetta's narrative and the discovery of important details that are missing in the mainstream version. The omissions include the explicit contentions, as well as implications. I also took into account Pigafetta's misinterpretations of certain events. Through an analysis and thoughtful reading of Pigafetta's narrative, I was able to connect the dots and bridge the gaps in the sequence of events, as well as put in place the missing parts of the puzzle. In the process, I learned the implications, understood the hidden meanings, and uncovered the untold story.

I found the underlying issues, motives, perceptions, struggles, conflicts, contradictions, and the games of deception that played out in the interactions between Magellan and the Austronesian natives of the islands through what both sides said, what was left unsaid, what they promised to do, and failed to deliver, what they did, and did not do, as well as the lies disguised as truth, and presented as benefits, cooperation, and/or compliance.

In the process of finding the untold story, I made discoveries that will significantly change and even debunk the mainstream version of the narrative of Magellan's arrival and death in the Philippines.

I discovered that Magellan had his own secret personal purpose and destination in undertaking the historic voyage. Moreover, Magellan's death in Mactan was the result of a well-planned native conspiracy that involved the unified participation of three Rajahs and the native warriors of the Vizzaya islands and Northern Mindanao.

Enrique, the Austronesian Interpreter

In my investigation, I considered the importance of the participation of Enrique, Magellan's interpreter and slave, whom Magellan acquired in Malacca in 1511 when Enrique was only 18 years old. From there, Magellan took Enrique to Portugal, then to Africa, back to Portugal, to Spain, and then on his historic voyage in 1519 from Spain bound for the Moluccas. Henrich, the Christian name given to him by Magellan, is described in Magellan's Last Will and Testament as a 26 year old Mulatto from Malacca. The word Mulatto defines Enrique as an Austronesian-Malay, someone with the genetic mixture of the black aboriginal inhabitants of Southeast Asia and the Mongolian-Chinese from mainland China.

Upon reaching the gold island of Mindanao, Enrique, who spoke Cebuano-Vizzaya took the very important role of Magellan's interpreter, a job that he did very well in all of Magellan's dealings, meetings, and conversations with the two Northern Mindanao kings; the Rajah of Mazzaua (Madjawa), and the Rajah of Butuan-Kalagan, their men, the people of Baug in the territory of Mazzaua, the Rajah of Cebu, the chiefs of Cebu, and the people of Cebu.

Enrique, in his role as interpreter, was knowledgeable in three languages: Portuguese, Spanish, and Cebuano. He effectively facilitated communications for three weeks between two parties: the natives (the Rajah of Mazzaua, the Rajah of Cebu, his chief men, the Cebuano people), and the Europeans (Magellan and his men).

Although Antonio Pigafetta was the journalist who wrote the eyewitness accounts of the events and the people of Magellan's voyage, without Enrique's help Pigafetta would not have been able to write a comprehensible narrative that included the recording of substantial verbal expressions and information from the natives.

The fact that Enrique spoke Cebuano, the lingua franca of the Vizzaya cultural region, must make him a native of the Vizzaya region of the pre-Philippine islands, an important detail that has been overlooked and disregarded in the mainstream version of Magellan's historic voyage as well as Pigafetta's narrative. I believe it is important to examine Enrique's role as Magellan's interpreter in the pre-Philippine gold islands, for it holds a significant insight into the untold story of Magellan's voyage.

Transforming Pigafetta's Story into History

While embracing Pigafetta's eyewitness account as the best and most credible source of information regarding the arrival of Magellan's voyage in the Philippines, this author acknowledges the fact that a direct unquestioning acceptance of Pigafetta's report without reflecting on its content is simply an encounter with raw narrative data. To transform Pigafetta's report into history, it is necessary to closely study, analyze, and synthesize the reported events and facts.

Simply taking Pigafetta's narrative account at face value, devoid of analysis, could easily lead to problems of misperceptions, erroneous comprehensions, and the creation of myths that advertently or inadvertently would be interpreted as historical truths. Although Pigafetta tried to write his chronicles with the independent point of view of a journalist, in some instances his writings reflect his bias in defense of Magellan's motives, actions, and character as well as his Roman Catholic values.

For example, while writing about Magellan's threats to the natives that in almost all instances preceded his attempt to convert them to Christianity, Pigafetta seems to implicitly justify the means that Magellan employed.

Spanish friars, who later in the 17th century AD would write their interpretations of Pigafetta's account, capitalized on Pigafetta's Christian bias. Their writings would find their way into the mainstream version which has portrayed Magellan as a Christian explorer turned overzealous missionary who died in battle while trying to convert into God's fold one stubborn pagan chief and his followers. This particular part of the narrative elevates Magellan into the status of a martyr, while at the same time downplaying or even negating the fact that Magellan was an invader who used religion in his attempt to subjugate and establish control over the natives.

A close analysis of the events and facts, however, shows that Magellan was a *conquistador* who employed a consistent pattern of both implicit and explicit serious verbal intimidations and threats against the natives, along with the imposition of the Christian religion, to drive fear into their hearts, and subjugate them. On this note, a point of interest that comes to attention is that although Pigafetta's account of Magellan's death in the kingdom of Cebu runs just a few paces short of Magellan's martyrdom, the narrative of Magellan's relationship with the natives that in the beginning seemed like a fairy tale, in the end, had morphed into a horror story.

Questions and Issues as Clues to the Untold Story

The quest for the untold story of Magellan's voyage in the pre-Philippines involves serious consideration of the questions and issues regarding the voyage. Certain inconsistencies, aberrations, and anomalies inherent in the unfolding of the events in the mainstream version trigger questions and the examination of issues that lead to new insights and the discovery of unforeseen truths.

Hidden, unnoticed, and unreported, these truths and insights offer a new version of Magellan's voyage in the pre-Philippines with new implications and revelations regarding this chapter of world history.

The Purpose of Magellan's Voyage

The first question focuses on the official purpose of the voyage, which was to find a westward route to the Moluccas. Did Magellan intend to pursue the official purpose of the voyage when he reached the pre-Philippines? Upon reaching the pre-Philippine gold islands, Magellan deviated from the known and stated purpose of the voyage, and embarked on a series of actions that show that he had a hidden agenda, a secret personal purpose for going on such an expedition. Magellan's paradigm shift would trigger a native conspiracy against him that resulted in his death and the debacle of his voyage in the pre-Philippines.

The Inclusion of Enrique, the Interpreter

The second question is about Enrique, the Malay interpreter. Why did Magellan take a slave and interpreter who spoke Cebuano, the language of the pre-Philippine gold islands? During the Portuguese invasion and conquest of Malacca in 1511, Magellan acquired Enrique, a teenage warrior who became his interpreter when ten years later his voyage from Spain reached the pre-Philippines in Southeast Asia.

Enrique was a "captured slave" indicating that Enrique was not bought in a slave market by Magellan. He may have been one of the defenders of the city who was taken captive in the final Portuguese assault in 1511. Prisoners of war would have been regarded as slaves and could be divided as booty among the officers and men of the victorious Portuguese expedition.

He may also have been a slave before the fall of the city. There were thousands of slaves in Melaka belonging to merchants and the Malay nobility. Portuguese records indicate that Sultan Mahmud of Melaka alone had over three thousand 'ambarages' ('Hamba Raja' or royal slaves). Many of the "hamba raja" were in fact prisoners of war brought back from Melaka's successful campaigns against the kingdom of Sumatra."

(http://sabrizain .org/Malay/port 3.htm).

Pigafetta, on page 67 of his account, refers to Enrique as Magellan's slave from Zamatra (Sumatra), formerly called Traprobana, but Enrique spoke Cebuano, the *lingua franca* of the Vizzaya cultural region of the Vizzaya islands and Mindanao in the Philippines. One possible scenario is that Enrique was abducted by Moro slave traders from one of the small islands in the kingdom of Cebu and sold as a slave warrior in Sumatra, then later ended up as a royal slave in Melaka (Malacca).

The inclusion of Enrique as speaking Cebuano, the language of the Vizzaya cultural region in the pre-Philippines, also triggers a very important question. If the destination of the voyage was the Moluccas, why did Magellan employ an interpreter who spoke the language of the pre-Philippine gold islands? Besides, if Magellan's real intended destination was the Moluccas, it was not necessary for him to get an interpreter. His good friend, Francisco Serrao, whose ship and men were accidentally stranded in the Moluccas in 1511, ended up as mercenaries in the service of a Moluccan king. Getting a local interpreter in the Moluccas would not be an issue if and when Magellan's voyage arrived there.

Revisiting the story of Magellan's participation in the 1511 Portuguese invasion and conquest of Malacca, where he acquired his Malay-Austronesian interpreter, provides a valuable key in unlocking the door to Magellan's secret motive for envisioning, planning, and embarking on the historic voyage.

Magellan's Defeat and Death in Mactan

Magellan's defeat and death in the battle of Mactan was a terrible aberration that raises a serious question. It was non-sequitur in the language of logic. The conclusion failed to follow the logical sequence of events, which leads us to a third question. How did this aberration happen? By all military considerations, Magellan and his men had an unfair advantage in the battle against the natives. The Europeans were equipped with superior arms and firepower. The large artillery of the mighty cannons from their ships could without doubt effectively demolish the native warriors and their territory. Magellan and his men were armed with guns, crossbows, and swords against the natives with their bolos (broad thick swords), bamboo spears, bows and arrows, and wicker shields. Magellan and his soldiers had metal shields, and wore protective metal armor. The native warriors were practically naked, their bare bodies covered only with tattoos, and 'bahag' loin cloths.

Making this scenario even more disconcerting is the fact that Magellan was not at war with the whole kingdom of Cebu. Rajah Humabon, the king, his chieftains, and their followers submitted without incident to Christian baptism, and were supposed to be Magellan's loyal followers and friends. With their baptism, these people pledged loyalty to the Emperor of Spain, and showed cooperation, obedience, and friendship towards Magellan and his men. Magellan went to war only against one man, Datu Si Lapu-Lapu, a renegade Cebuano chief of Mactan Island. Yet Magellan was killed after ordering his men to retreat and flee from the scene of the battle. How was this possible?

The Massacre of Magellan's Survivors

As if the aberration of Magellan's death was not enough, four days later, twenty one of his men were massacred in the square outside the palace of Rajah Humabon, the King of Cebu

13

who had invited them to lunch. Why did Rajah Humabon and his warriors carry out this horrific massacre? Humabon was supposed to be their loyal friend and ally. During their three-week stay in the kingdom of Cebu, Rajah Humabon had shown them only cooperation and friendship. In fact, Pigafetta proudly referred to him as the Christian King. Humabon was the first native king or rajah who was baptized.

In a desperate attempt to make sense of the massacre of Magellan's survivors, Pigafetta points to a conspiracy implicating Enrique, the interpreter. Pigafetta was right about a conspiracy, but the conspiracy that he wrote about was the mere tail end of a native conspiracy with a much broader origin, scope, and participation than he had come to realize.

Pigafetta was also wrong about Enrique's involvement in the conspiracy. His realization of a conspiracy miserably fails to adequately explain the unbelievable defeat and death of Magellan in the battle of Mactan, as well as the involvement of Rajah Humabon in the bloody massacre of Magellan's men in the square outside his palace four days after Magellan's death.

Getting to the bottom of these questions, issues, and bizarre events in Pigafetta's eyewitness account reveals the untold story of Magellan's voyage in the pre-Philippines. The details and their significance will be presented in the context of the discussion that follows.

Breaking the Code of Pigafetta's Chronicles

A close examination of Antonio Pigafetta's eyewitness account of the voyage yields significant information that has stayed hidden in the dark pages of history for centuries. An analysis of the facts, events, and circumstances concerning Magellan's dealings with the pre-Philippine natives, Killing Magellan *in the Pre-Philippine Gold Islands: The Untold Conspiracy and Beyond* unlocks the meanings and implications of the interactions between Magellan and the natives using as the primary source the eyewitness account of Antonio Pigafetta, the Italian chronicler of Magellan's voyage. His book is titled *Magellan's Voyage, A Narrative Account of the First Circumnavigation.* The most complete version of Pigafetta's surviving manuscripts is called the Yale-Beinecke Codex, published in 1969, written in French and translated into English by R.A. Skelton, a former superintendent of the British Museum. Pigafetta wrote the original chronicles of the voyage in Italian, titled *Relazione del Primo Viaggio Intorno al Mondo.* Later, Pigafetta wrote the French version which he presented to the Grandmaster of Rhodes, a Frenchman.

The process of uncovering the untold story started with the baffling issues and questions regarding Magellan's voyage in the pre-Philippines. Some of the issues involved things such as Magellan's paradigm shift from the official purpose of the voyage. They offer clues regarding Magellan's secret personal motive behind his ambition to lead and take on such a daunting challenge, and the unknown risks of a voyage no one before him had ever taken. What made him take the unimaginable risks, the high probability of losing his life, the lives of his crew, and the investment that the Emperor Charles V, and the other Spanish investors, had spent to finance the voyage? Magellan's deviation from the official purpose of the voyage upon reaching the Philippine gold islands, which even Magellan's survivors considered irrational, offers explanations and answers to these questions.

Pigafetta's eyewitness account contains considerable, significant information which sheds light on the disconcerting aberrations, anomalies and inconsistencies in the mainstream version written by Spanish friars and historians. Important events in Pigafetta's chronicles, excluded from the mainstream version, provide the explanations that put logic where it is absent, and make sense of the absurd in the mainstream version.

Gross omissions in the popular Spanish versions have resulted in a significant departure from Pigafetta's account of the portrayal of Magellan and the native kings, as well as their actions and interactions with each other. Likewise, some important events and places visited by Magellan were left out, resulting in a skewed narrative in favor of the Spanish colonial agenda. For example, the Spanish colonial version of the story has advertently or inadvertently omitted Magellan's visit and stay in Northern Mindanao, his meetings with Rajah Kalambu, the Rajah of Butuan-Kalagan and his brother, Rajah Si Ayo, the Rajah of Mazzaua who a week later escorted Magellan's fleet to the Rajahnate of Cebu. The exclusion of the Northern Mindanao episode has conveniently removed important events that started and led to the native conspiracy against Magellan, initiated by Rajah Si Ayo and Rajah Kalambu in Northern Mindanao, and continued in Cebu.

Never mentioning Magellan's serious threats of war against the natives, the Spaniards made it appear as if Rajah Humabon, the king of Cebu, and hundreds of his people had willingly and happily agreed to be baptized into the Catholic faith. The mass baptism of 800 Cebu natives in one day alone had been touted by the Spanish colonizers as the natives' realization of the superiority of Catholicism over their indigenous spiritual beliefs and practices.

A big troublesome thorn in the side of the otherwise smooth Spanish version of the narrative, however, is the fact that in spite of the supposed mass conversion and cooperation of the natives, two weeks later Magellan ended up dead on the shore of a little island off Cebu while launching a war of aggression to subdue into submission supposedly just one renegade chief, Si Lapu-Lapu, the Chief of Mactan. Since it was impossible to deny Magellan's unbelievable defeat and death in a war against the natives, the Spaniards had to invent a narrative that would somehow fit the premise of their story, however contrived it might be. Rather than focus on the fact that Magellan was a *conquistador*, the Spanish version portrays Magellan more as a missionary who had died trying to convert into God's fold one wild stubborn pagan native chief and his followers.

The most serious omission in the mainstream version of the narrative, however, is the massacre of twenty-two of Magellan's men in the courtyard of Rajah Humabon's palace in Cebu, four days after Magellan was killed on the island of Mactan. Magellan's men went ashore upon the invitation of Rajah Humabon, to eat lunch and to collect the tribute and gifts of gold ornaments that the Rajah had promised to send to the Emperor of the Spanish Empire. Until then, Rajah Humabon was supposed to be friendly towards Magellan and his crew, the first native king of the islands who had been baptized, and had willingly embraced Christianity, with a pledge of loyalty to the Emperor of Spain.

Denial of the Natives' Humanity

The Spanish friars had also neglected any attempt to include in their version of the story the socio-cultural, political, and historical conditions of 16th century indigenous Philippine society, resulting in the erroneous portrayal of the natives as devoid of historical personality and lacking any significant contributions towards the advancement of human civilization. The Spaniards called the natives salvajes (savages), implying that they were primitive, uncivilized, and an inferior people, a categorical denial of the natives' humanity.

On the contrary, Pigafetta, the eyewitness, wrote the chronicles with the relatively independent point of view of a journalist, as much as he could within a limited time. He wrote about their culture, their political system, their religion, the natural resources of their country or kingdom, their agricultural products, and domestic animals. In Cebu he wrote about the natives' homes with rooms which he described as like theirs in Europe. Pigafetta took special note of the friendly, hospitable native people of goodwill, and the indigenous society where they lived in peace and justice. Most notable of all is Pigafetta's account of the palace of the Rajah of Butuan-Kalagan which he described as having parts made of gold, as well as the rajah's receptacles of gold.

In the process of breaking the code of Pigafetta's chronicles, other sources were also referenced to support, clarify, and corroborate both Pigafetta's account and this author's insights. To make Pigafetta's narrative more comprehensible, it was necessary and helpful to analyze the events of Pigafetta's story within the context of 16th century Philippine society and culture, and its place in the general history of Southeast Asia before and during that time. The influence of the socio-cultural and historical conditions on the psychological mindset and behavior of the natives towards Magellan and his men is a dynamic that was also considered.

The inclusion of the story of Magellan's participation in the 1511 Portuguese invasion and conquest of Malacca, where he captured a Malay mulatto warrior who became his interpreter, also provides a crucial key in unlocking the door to Magellan's secret motive for envisioning, planning, and leading the historic voyage.

The Untold Story in 16th Century pre-Philippine Context

A careful reading and in-depth analysis of Antonio Pigafetta's eyewitness account, and interpreting it in the context of 16th century pre-Philippine society and of the Vizzaya cultural region, helps to reveal the untold story of Magellan's voyage in the pre-Philippines. A deeper look into Pigafettas's report, the sequence of events, Magellan's and the natives' words, actions, and interactions within the context of 16th century pre-Philippine society and culture uncovers the first united native conspiracy against a foreign invader in the gold islands, known to the ancient Greeks as Chryse. Likewise, understanding the pre-Philippine natives, their ancient origins and history that lead to the social, cultural, and political conditions in the 16th century, and their historical relations with their neighbors in Asia and Southeast Asia, was significantly helpful in making sense of the native's reaction to Magellan's arrival in their homeland.

Not mentioned in both the mainstream Spanish version and Pigafetta's account of Magellan's voyage in the pre-Philippines, the origins, culture, and history of the Austronesian-Malay people that Magellan encountered sheds significant light on the true but untold story about how the natives responded to Magellan's attempt to subjugate them, and to take control of their territory, lives and destiny. To say the least, Magellan was ill-prepared to deal with the Austronesian-Malay people in the gold islands, whose civilization and history dated back thousands of years before the emergence of European civilization.

The process of unlocking the code of Pigafetta's chronicles, as well as the origins and history of the Austronesian-Malay people, involved referencing the studies and research made by experts in archaelogy, genetics, anthropology, osteology, geology, linguistics, ethno-archaelogy, and history. I also took into consideration the folk literature and oral traditions of the Austronesian-Malay people whom Magellan encountered in the pre-Philippines.

CHAPTER I

PRELUDE TO MAGELLAN'S VOYAGE

"The more you know about the past, the better prepared you are for the future."- Theodore Roosevelt

Magellan in Malacca

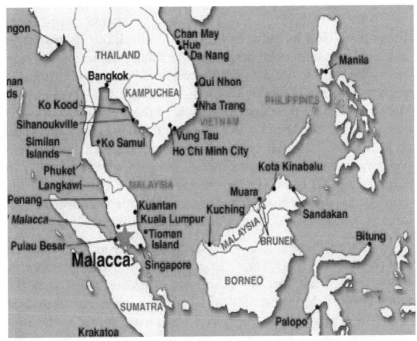

Fernao Magalhaes (anglicized as Ferdinand Magellan) was a Portuguese soldier who participated in the Portuguese invasion of the Sultanate of Malacca, also known as Melaka, a city-state in what is now Malaysia. Malacca, in those days, was the richest port and the biggest trading center in Southeast Asia due to its strategic location. Situated on the Strait of Malacca, the port was close to the Indian Ocean, providing relatively easy trade access to and from China and other kingdoms and countries in the Asia-Pacific Region as well as India, Arabia, Africa, and Europe.

Cloves and mace were among Malacca's most coveted trading products. For at least a century the spice trade and gold had attracted Asian, Arab and European traders to its port.

In 1400 a Malay nobleman, Sri Majara, the last Rajah of Singapura (Singapore), also known by the names Iskandar Shah (Alexander Shah) and Parameswara, founded the Sultanate of Malacca. (Wikipedia, Malacca, p.2).

In 1509, the Portuguese king sent a reconnaissance expedition from Goa in India to Malacca to check out its resources and level of commercial activities. Magellan was among the soldiers who went to Malacca on this mission. While the Portuguese ships were being loaded with goods, the warriors of the Sultan of Malacca attacked the Portuguese, whom they suspected of dubious motives other than trade. Although the Portuguese ended up retreating and leaving behind 19 of their men, the expedition confirmed that Malacca was indeed the prime trading center in Southeast Asia. Located close to the Indian Ocean, it was the gateway to Africa, the Middle East, and Europe. (Wikipedia, Malacca Sultanate: Portuguese Invasion and its Effects, (2011) p.5).

Among many diverse products, spices from the Moluccas that were worth their weight in gold were traded in Malacca. A commodity at the port of equal if not of greater value with the much-coveted Moluccan spices was gold itself. An abundant source of this gold was Northern Mindanao, south of the pre-Philippine islands. Butuan, the main trading port, was part of the Chinese Nanhai South Seas and Southeast Asian Sri Vijaya trading network from the 7th - 13th century AD. The Butuan Port was still an international port in the 16th century.

On April 1511, from Goa in Western India, the Portuguese king sent a fleet of 18 ships under the command of Alfonso de Albuquerque to invade and conquer Malacca. During that period, Magellan had been in India, and he was among the soldiers who sailed with the Portuguese fleet to Malacca and participated in the invasion. His exceptional fighting skills as a soldier in the invasion of Malacca earned him a promotion to the rank of captain. Seven months after the start of the invasion, in November 1511, the Portuguese had completely conquered Malacca. (Wikipedia, Malacca Sultanate, (2011) p. 5)

Magellan Determines Voyage Destination:
The Pre-Philippine Gold Islands

In Malacca, Magellan would have known about the islands to the northeast as an abundant source of gold that was traded at the port. It was then that Magellan saw the opportunity to lead his own voyage of exploration and discovery to the islands of gold in Southeast Asia.

In ancient times, the islands in insular Southeast Asia were called Suvarnadbhumi, a Sanskrit term meaning "the Golden Land" (Wikipedia, Suvarnabhumi, (2015) p.1). The classical Greek geographer, Claudius Ptolemy gave the name Chryse meaning the Golden One to the pre-Philippines, the islands east of Khruses Kersonenson, the Golden Peninsula, now known as the Malay Peninsula (Encyclopedia Britannica, eb.com). The famed Port of Malacca was situated on the southern end of the Malay Peninsula.

In 1295 Marco Polo sailed with 14 Chinese junks from China to accompany a Chinese Princess to Persia to become the bride of Kublai Khan's grand nephew, who at that time ruled Persia (Marco Polo, Wikipedia). In his account of the voyage, Marco Polo wrote about crossing south to Vietnam, then to the Malay Peninsula "where gold is so plentiful that no one who did not see it could believe it" (The Explorer Marco Polo: Saudi Aramco World, Vol. 56, Number 4, July/August (2005).

John Burton, Professor of Xavier University in Cagayan de Oro in Mindanao, Philippines, wrote about Marco Polo's account in reference to the pre-Philippine gold islands:

"When Marco Polo began his homeward voyage from China to Venice in 1295, he made a special paragraph in his writings which must have referred to the Philippines. He said that 7, 444 islands lay to the east of China and were fully populated. They abounded in timber and spices and traded these products with one another. He then made a particular reference to a place rich in gold, washed down to the seashore by mighty rivers.

So big were the nuggets, he said, that by merely strolling in the sand one would kick them over with his feet." (Greg Hontiveros, Butuan of a Thousand Years, Butuan City Historical and Cultural Foundation, Inc. (2004) p.16)

The account of Antonio Pigafetta, Magellan's chronicler, in 1521, probably refers to the same place described by Marco Polo. Regarding the king of Butuan-Kalagan in Northern Mindanao, with its seat along the great Agusan River, Pigafetta wrote the following: "In the island of that king who came to the ship are mines of gold, which is found by digging from the earth large pieces as large as walnuts and eggs." Marco Polo's account is also echoed in Pigafetta's mention of the gold mines in the kingdom of Mazzaua. (Antonio Pigafetta, Magellan's Voyage, A Narrative Account of the First Circumnavigation, Trans. by R.A. Skelton, New York, Dover Publications (1969) p.69).

William Henry Scott suggests that Magellan probably came to know about the pre-Philippine gold islands during his stay in Malacca. Magellan most likely would have known of the gold in the homeland of the most valiant warriors of the Sultan of Malacca, the ancient explorers, discoverers, and the business tycoons who were from the pre-Philippines. Scott mentions as an example Regimo Diraja, a tycoon from the pre-Philippines, and owner of a large shipping and export business to China and other states in Southeast Asia. Scott wrote, *"Perhaps the 'discovery of the Philippines' was made in Malacca"* (Scott, 194).

Magellan Gets an Interpreter

Magellan seriously wanted to get to the islands of gold, and he needed someone who knew the language of the people of the islands. Considering the presence of a great number of people from the pre-Philippines who were then living, working, and even engaged in business in Malacca (Scott, 194), it would have been fairly easy to find a young slave-warrior who he could take with him on his planned voyage. "

Magellan found and took as his personal slave a particular teen-age Malayan boy for good reason. The boy could speak Cebuano, commonly known as Vijaya/Bisaya, the language of trade and diplomacy in the gold kingdoms of the pre-Philippine islands. *"The northern and eastern coasts of Mindanao were part of the Visayan culture area: from Surigao in the east to Sindangan Bay in the west, missionaries were able to make themselves under-stood in Cebuano"* (Scott, 161). Bisaya/Cebuano was widely spo-ken in the Vijaya/Vizzaya cultural region of the Vizzaya islands and Mindanao, which still holds true today.

Magellan Sails East From Malacca

Shortly after the conquest of Malacca, Magellan took a ship and sailed east without the permission of Captain-General Alfonso de Albuquerque (Wikipedia, Ferdinand Magellan, p. 2). Magellan was supposed to have reached Sabah in Northern Bor-neo. Was this Magellan's first attempt to sail towards the pre-Philippine islands? This possibility is not remote because the pre-Philippines, as it would later turn out, were a major if not the most important part of his plans for a later expedition. Magellan took an excursion from Malacca to the pre-Philippine islands perhaps to know its exact location and confirm that indeed it was rich in gold. When Magellan's ship came close to the coast of Northern Borneo, Magellan might have spotted Bornean pirate ships. He had no choice but to turn back towards Malacca, al-though when he reached Borneo he had in fact come very close to the gold islands. Sabah in Borneo is just 29 kilometers from the Sulu islands in the Philippines, which are 926 kilometers by sea to the Butuan Port in Northern Mindanao, the richest source of gold.

As a result of his unlicensed reconnaissance trip towards Borneo, Captain-General Albuquerque stripped Magellan of his rank, and forced him to leave Malacca in 1512 (Wikipedia, Ferdi-nand Magellan, 1).

In spite of his failed attempt to reach the Land of Gold, Magellan never lost his resolve to get there one way or another.

Magellan's plan to lead a voyage of exploration and discovery on a westward route to the Moluccas, by several considerations, was probably made in Malacca. It was in Malacca that Magellan would have learned about the pre-Philippine islands as an abundant source of the gold that was traded at the port of the kingdom. Since Malacca was the leading Southeast Asian trading center in the 16th century, the flow of goods, raw materials, forest and agricultural products came to the port from all over Southeast Asia, China, Indo-China, and India. Large quantities of gold ore and finished gold products from Northeastern Mindanao, which were traded at the port of the Butuan-Kalagan kingdom, would have found their way to Malacca.

For centuries, the Butuan Port was part of the Nanhai (South Seas) trading network in Southeast Asia, long before the coming of the Europeans. This network from China operated with the Sri Vijaya, the maritime Empire centered in Sumatra that controlled the sea lanes and trade routes in Southeast Asia from the 7th – 13th centuries.

Magellan's desire to reach the gold islands must have been the motive behind his plan to lead an expedition on a route no one before him had ever taken. He knew if he could find a westward route to the Moluccas, he would get to the pre-Philippine gold islands along the way, somewhere on the eastern shores of the Pacific Ocean. Like Columbus, Almeida, and Albuquerque before him, Magellan wanted to launch his own voyage of exploration, discovery, and territorial conquest. He would be the first European explorer to reach the pre-Philippine gold islands.

Magellan Leaves Malacca

Magellan left Malacca sometime in 1512, taking Enrique with him back to Portugal. Later, in 1513, Enrique was with Magellan when he went to Morocco and fought in the

Battle of Azamor. While in Morocco, Magellan was accused of illegal trading with the Moors, and of corruption (Wikipedia, Ferdinand Magellan, 1).

Magellan's non-commissioned trip to the east of Malacca, and his questionable dealings with Moors in Morocco are events that offer important insights into a significant side of Magellan's character. These two actions by Magellan show that he was a maverick with an independent streak. He had the will and the tendency to circumvent the rules and defy authority to get what he wanted. He was fearless, with a strong spirit of adventure and conquest. These traits motivated him to plan a voyage on a route no one before him had ever taken, with a secret purpose known only to himself.

CHAPTER II

VOYAGE PROPOSALS, PURPOSE & DESTINATION

"The brutal history of colonialism is one in which white people literally stole land, and people for their own gain and material wealth."

– Patrisse Cullors

King Manuel I Rejects Magellan's Proposal

Upon his return to Portugal from Morocco, Magellan offered his proposal to find a westward route to the Moluccas to King Manuel I, the King of Portugal. Given Magellan's record of dodging authority and breaking the rules during his stint in Malacca, as well as engaging in illegal trade with the Moors in Morocco, King Manuel I rejected Magellan's proposal. Although the charges against Magellan were later dropped, King Manuel refused to give Magellan a pay raise. In fact, King Manuel I informed Magellan that his employment would cease after May 15, 1514. Disgruntled upon King Manuel's rejection, and the gloomy prospect of unemployment in Portugal, Magellan set his sights on Spain. In 1517, Magellan left Portugal and went to the Spanish City of Seville. During the European Age of Exploration, Seville was the center of ideas that attracted all kinds of men from all over Europe who dreamed of exploration, discovery, and adventure. (Wikipedia, Ferdinand Magellan, 2)

The King of Spain Accepts Magellan's Proposal

Shortly after his arrival in Seville, Magellan met and married Beatriz de Barbosa, a Spanish woman whose Portuguese father had strong connections to the Spanish nobility. It is said during this time that Magellan became a Spanish citizen. Having a Spanish wife from an influential family, Magellan gained respectability and a credible status within the higher ranks of Spanish socio-political circles, through which he obtained access to Charles V, the king of Spain (Wikipedia, Ferdinand Magellan, 2, 3)

Magellan offered his proposal to the young eighteen-year -old King Charles V who approved it in 1518. In June 1519, Pope Leo X elected Charles V Emperor of the Holy Roman Empire. (Pigafetta, 7).

The Official Purpose of the Voyage

In Magellan's proposal, the purpose of his voyage was not to circumnavigate the world, but to find a westward route to the Moluccas, the fabled Spice Islands in Southeast Asia. Emperor Charles V approved Magellan's proposal, and with other investors funded the expedition under Magellan's command to sail to the Moluccas "by way of the west and discover that which until now has not been found within our demarcation." (Pigafetta, 1, 7).

Open to the bold ideas of exploration that came with the Age of Exploration and Discovery, the young king of Spain and his court shared the excitement of the prospect of discovering a westward route to the Moluccas. Magellan's fearless and daring proposal impressed King Charles V. The proposal offered the Spanish Empire the opportunity to find a westward ocean route to Southeast Asia – an urgent issue for Spain, because the control of the eastward route through the Indian Ocean was already given to Portugal in the Treaty of Torsedillas. If discovered, the westward route would come under Spain's dominion and definitely establish a competitive edge over Portugal, Spain's rival in the discovery and conquest of new territories outside of Europe during the Age of Exploration.

The June 7, 1494 Treaty of Torsedillas, an agreement between Spain and Portugal, drew a demarcation line from the top to the bottom of the globe. Places both discovered and undiscovered east of the demarcation line would belong to Portugal, and places west of the demarcation to Spain. Magellan's official objective was to sail to the Moluccas in Southeast Asia through a westward route, and to find places west of the demarcation line to claim for the Spanish empire.

Moluccas: The Official Destination of Magellan's Voyage

The Moluccas, also known as the Spice Islands, are east of Sulawesi, and north of East Timor in the Indonesian islands in Southeast Asia. In relation to its neighbors, the Moluccas are northeast of Malacca, southeast of the Philippines, and lie northwest of New Guinea. In the sixteenth century, the Europeans considered as valuable as gold the spices such as cloves and nutmeg that grew only in the Moluccas. China, India, the pre-Philippine Islands, Malacca, Java, Japan, Singhapura (Singapore), Vietnam, Cambodia, Thailand, and some Arabian countries also participated in the lucrative spice trade from the Moluccas.

Magellan's Hidden Personal Agenda

Besides the official purpose of the voyage, however, Magellan had a secret mission which he had kept all to himself. Finding a westward route to the Moluccas was without question revolutionary, and consistent with the doctrine of exploration and discovery. As such, its significance was an effective cover for Magellan's personal motives for taking the voyage. Magellan wanted to follow that route because he knew that his voyage would take him to the islands of gold, northeast of the Malay Archipelago.

While the known and stated purpose of Magellan's voyage was to reach the Moluccas, the Spice Islands, unbeknownst to everybody else Magellan had a hidden personal purpose: to find and conquer the pre-Philippine gold islands.

Magellan's Secret Destination:
The pre-Philippine Gold Islands

The country of Butuan-Kalagan in northern Mindanao in the pre-Philippines was Magellan's secret destination, although he still had to find it. Having known of the Land of Gold northeast of Malacca, Magellan was determined to take his voyage to this rich source of gold in Southeast Asia. Magellan knew that by taking a westward route to the Moluccas across the Pacific Ocean, he had a good chance of finding the pre-Philippine gold islands, northwest of the Moluccas. It was a wild but calculated guess which, after undertaking a voyage of unimaginable risks, proved Magellan right.

Magellan's Voyage Departs from Spain

Magellan's fleet of five ships and 237 men left Spain from the Port of San Lucar de Barrameda on September 20, 1519. The five ships sailed across the Atlantic to Brazil, then along the eastern coast of South America. They continued to sail south to Argentina where they stayed at the Port of San Julian for several months. Fourteen months later, in Southern Chile, they found a strait (later named the Magellan Strait) that connects the Atlantic Ocean to the Pacific Ocean. Only three ships were left: the flagship Trinidad, the Victoria, and the Concepcion. One ship was lost at sea near the Port of San Julian in Argentina, and the Santo Antonio secretly went back to Spain right after the discovery of the Magellan Strait. On November 28, 1520, the three remaining ships entered the Pacific Ocean (Pigafetta, 40-57).

The Voyage Reaches Guam

After three months and twenty days of sailing across the Pacific Ocean, Magellan's fleet of three ships reached Guam in the South Pacific on March 6, 1521.

When they anchored close to the shores of Guam, they were unable to get provisions. The natives entered their ships, robbed them, and stole one of their skiffs. Pigafetta wrote that Magellan's men were so weak and emaciated from hunger and disease, they were unable to stop the natives. Magellan was so angered that he took forty of his men on a small skiff. When they landed on the island, they burned fifty houses and boats, killed seven men and recovered the skiff. Leaving Guam, which they called **Islas de Ladrones**, (the Islands of Thieves), they sailed farther west (Pigafetta, 58, 59).

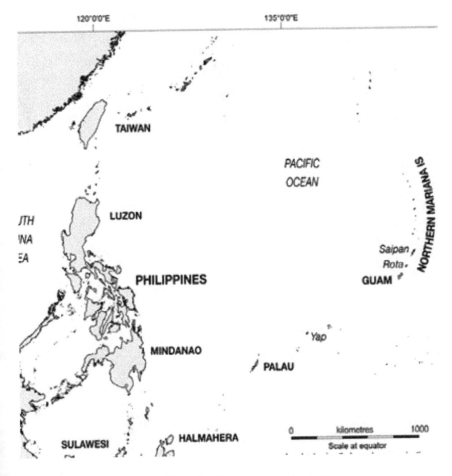

Photo Credit: www.researchgate.net

CHAPTER III

MAGELLAN'S VOYAGE REACHES
THE PRE-PHILIPPINES

"Study the past if you would define the future." - Confucius

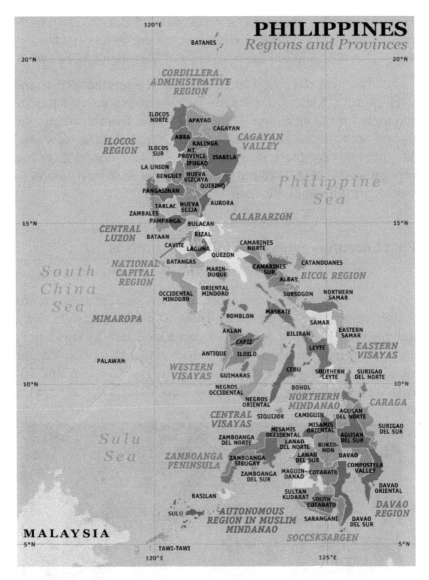

Present day Map of the Philippines

On March 16, 1521, Magellan's voyage reached the shores of the pre-Philippine Islands, 108 days after crossing the Pacific Ocean from the western coast of South America.

At daybreak, they anchored near the island of Zzamal (Samar) in the Eastern Vijaya (Vizzaya) Region of the pre-Philippine Islands. This date marked the beginning of Magellan's last days.

The next day, they anchored near the uninhabited island of Humunu (Homonhon) where they went ashore and put up two tents for the sick men. There they found fresh drinking water, coconut trees, and wild boars. They caught a sow and slaughtered it for food. Magellan chose to stop and rest on this unpopulated island. Without having to deal with any natives, it was safer for him and his men.

First Encounter with pre-Philippine Natives

Two days later, nine ornately dressed men from the neighboring island of Zzuluan (Suluan) came. Through signs, and gestures, the most ornately-dressed indicated he was happy about the coming of Magellan's fleet, an expression of diplomatic friendship. For the first time in the voyage, Magellan and his men came face-to-face with Austronesian-Malay natives from the islands.

Manobo Men in Traditional Clothing

Photo Credit: *Leo Esclanda/*GMA News

The native men brought fish, a jar of palm wine, figs (bananas) a foot long, and two coconuts. Upon seeing the good-will of the natives, Magellan gave the men gifts of mirrors, combs, bells, boccasins and other things. Again through signs and gestures, they told Magellan that they would return in four days with rice, coconuts, and other kinds of food. True to their promise, the natives returned four days later, this time with their chieftain in two boats loaded with "coconuts, sweet oranges, a jar of palm wine, and a cock." Magellan graciously paid for these provisions (Pigafetta, 65).

The First Signs of Gold

Magellan and his men saw their first signs of gold, as noted by Pigafetta in his description of the Chief of Zzuluan and his men: "The Lord of those people was old, and had his face painted, and he wore hanging from his ears golden rings which they call Schione, and the others wore many gold bracelets and armlets, with linen kerchief on their head." (Pigafetta, 65).

Writing about the Caphri (Kapri) people on another nearby island, Pigafetta wrote, "Those people are brown, fat and painted...they have very black hair hanging to their waist, and they wear small daggers and knives, and lances adorned with gold."

Besides the gold-adorned bodies and implements of the natives, Pigafetta also took special notice of the tattoos. Pigafetta thought the tattoos on the natives' bodies were designs painted on their skin. The ancient Austronesian art of tattooing was obviously new, foreign, and even strange to Pigafetta, and the other Europeans on Magellan's voyage.

Magellan Threatens the Samar Natives Regarding the Source of the Gold

"These people entered into very great familiarity and friendship with us, and made us understand several things in their language and the names of some islands which we saw before us. The island in which they lived is called Zzuluan, which is not very large. We took great pleasure with them because they were merry and conversible. The captain seeing that they were well-disposed, to do them more honor, led them to his ship and showed them all his merchandise, cloves, cinnamon, pepper, walnut, ginger, mace, gold, and all that was in the ship. He also caused his artillery to fire several times, whereat they were much afraid, so that they tried to leap from the ship into the sea.

And they made signs that the things which the captain had shown them grew in the places whither we were going."

(Pigafetta, 64).

An in-depth reading of the preceding incident presents certain diplomatic and political implications. The natives' show of goodwill and friendship, while maybe genuine, was definitely part of diplomatic protocol. When the Zzuluan natives first came in a boat to meet with Magellan and his men on the uninhabited island of Homonhon, they came in their most ornate formal outfits and gold accessories to show that they were dressed for a formal diplomatic meeting with the foreigners. Otherwise, everyday casual native wear consisted of bare tattooed bodies with loin cloths or g-strings called 'bahag', the sensible daily outfit in the hot and humid tropical weather of the islands.

By showing the natives the spices and gold on his ship, Magellan wanted to know from the natives the sources of such goods on the islands. Due to a communication gap, or reticence on the part of the natives, Magellan fired the artillery from the cannons of his ship to shake the information out of the natives. The strategy worked, because after the artillery was fired, the terrified natives told Magellan through signs and gestures that those spices and gold are found in the south, directing them towards the big island of Mindanao. By doing so, the natives also implicitly encouraged the foreigners to stay away. The reticence of the natives, who might have pretended that they were unable to understand Enrique, the interpreter, could also be interpreted as the Zzuluan natives' way of limiting or even withholding information that Magellan wanted from them. This could be the first sign of native resistance against the arrival of Magellan's voyage in the pre-Philippine islands.

Going for the Gold, Literally

Nine days after their arrival, Magellan's fleet left the island of Homonhon. On Monday, the 25th of March, they sailed going in a direction between west and southwest through the Surigao Strait. Along the way, they passed in the midst of five islands, Cenalo (present-day North Dinagat Islands), Hinanggar (Hinunangan), Hibusson, (Ibusson) and Abarien (northern Leyte). Some of these islands are bigger than Homonhon or Zzuluan, yet they did not stop at any of them. With his fleet, Magellan sailed with a singular purpose in mind. They were on their way to the island of gold, and they had to get there quick.

Magellan's Ships

CHAPTER IV

MAGELLAN'S VOYAGE IN MAZZAUA, NORTHERN MINDANAO

"The more you know of your history, the more liberated you are."

– Maya Angelou

Offshore in Malimono, Mazzaua

Three days later, on March 28, 1521, they anchored close to the shores of Malimono, on the west coast of northern Surigao, north of Mindanao. The night before, they saw fire on that island. The "fire" could have been the bright light of extremely large swarms of fireflies that inhabit certain trees and plants in the rich mangrove forests along the rivers and seashores of northeastern Mindanao. *"On Thursday, twenty eighth of March, because during the night we had seen fire on the island ahead, we came to anchor near the said island, where we saw a small boat called Baloto with eight men in it, which came near to the captain-general's ship"* (Pigafetta, 67).

"That island is in the latitude of nine and two-thirds degrees toward the Arctic Pole, and in the longitude of one hundred sixty-two from the line of demarcation. And from the other island, where we found springs of fresh water, it is 25 leagues distant. And that island is called Mazzaua" (Pigafetta, 72). Altough Pigafetta was not a trained navigator, he must have obtained the navigational coordinates from Francisco Albo, the pilot of the Trinidad, Captain-General Magellan's ship, the lead ship of the voyage. Pigafetta as the chronicler, and Enrique, the interpreter were also on the Trinidad.

Enrique the Interpreter Speaks Cebuano

Enrique, Magellan's Cebuano-speaking interpreter, spoke to the natives on the boat and they appeared to understand him. *"Then a slave of his who was of Zamatra, formerly called Traprobana, spoke to those at a distance, and they heard him speak and came alongside the ship, but drew off quickly, and would not come on board because they mistrusted us. Then the captain seeing their mistrust, showed them a red cap and other things, which he caused to be tied and fastened on a small plank, which those of the boat took forthwith and gladly, and then returned to inform their king."* (Pigafetta, 67).

First Appearance of the Rajah of Mazzaua (Madjawa)

"Two hours or so later we saw approaching two long boats which they call Ballanghai, full of men, and in the larger was their king seated below an awning made of mats. And when they came near the captain's ship, the said slave spoke to that king, who understood him well. For in that country, the kings know more languages than people do" (Pigafetta, 67).

The king on the balanghai (balangay) boat was the Rajah of Mazzaua. He understood Enrique, who spoke to him in Cebuano. For the first time since they had reached the pre-Philippine Islands, the interpreter was able to communicate in a spoken language with the natives. While it could be true that the kings knew more languages than their subjects, it was not the case with the Chief of Zzuluan, who with his men communicated only through signs and gestures.

The Rajah of Mazzaua Offers Magellan a Gift of Gold

"Then the king ordered some of his men to go to the captain's ship, (telling him that he would not stir from his boat rather close to us). Which he did, and when his men returned to his boat, he immediately departed. The captain made good cheer to those who came to the ship and gave them many things. Wherefore the king wished to give the captain a bar of massy gold, of a good size and a basket full of ginger. But the captain thanking him greatly refused to accept the present" (Pigafetta, 67).

Massy gold is raw gold ore. Pigafetta's preceding account marks the beginning of Magellan's journey into the gold kingdoms of Mazzaua and Butuan-Kalagan in northern Mindanao. The king on the ballanghai (balangay) boat was Rajah Siaiu (Si Ayo), the King of the Rajanate or Kingdom of Mazzaua (pronounced Ma-djaw-a). The eight native men who first came in a small boat were the king's men who were sent to check out Magellan's fleet. Without hiding their mistrust for Magellan and his men, who they thought were probably foreign invaders, the natives were wary of those who had come into their territory. Knowing that foreign invasion was a real possibility, they had to consider their options.

Drawing from the civilized traditions of a rajahnate, Rajah Si Ayo approached the situation with diplomacy instead of hostility. He offered Magellan a gift as a sign of peace. The gift was a good-sized bar of gold ore. For what could be a more suitable royal gift than gold, the metal of the gods, and the most valuable asset of the kingdom? Magellan, however, refused to accept the bar of gold ore. A tactical move on his part, Magellan held back from showing any sign of interest in the gold. He wanted to keep his desire for the gold to himself to prevent raising any red flags that would have certainly alarmed the natives, and would ruin his later, bigger plans.

Magellan in fact maintained this astute, indifferent attitude involving gold transactions with the natives throughout their eight-day stay in northern Mindanao. Magellan's refusal to accept the king's gift of gold, however, would have raised a question in the king's mind. Did Magellan's refusal mean a rejection of the king's offer of peace? The king, then, would have seen the need for more caution in dealing with Magellan.

Balangay Boats to Baug

Following the initial contact with Magellan, Rajah Si Ayo and his men immediately left in the two balangay boats, and headed south. Magellan's fleet followed the king's boats towards Butuan. *"Then in the evening we came with the ships near to the captain's house".* (Pigafetta, 67). Pigafetta refers to Rajah Si Ayo as a captain. True to Austronesian sea-faring tradition, as well as the requirements of his position and rank as king, Rajah Si Ayo also had to be an expert navigator and captain.

Suspicious of Magellan's ships that were following them, the king's balangay boats stopped on the shore of Baug an island along Butuan Bay. (Gabriel B. Atega, Where is Mazzawa? Sweet Tree Inc. (2010) p.9). From offshore Malimono, in Surigao, it was evening when they reached the shores of Baug which was part of the Rajahnate of Mazzaua. It takes about three hours to sail from Northern Surigao to Butuan Bay in Northern Agusan.

Magellan's ships anchored close by. The island of Baug is seven kilometers (three miles) downstream from the Butuan Port, and the palace of the King of Butuan-Kalagan situated on one of the islands along the interior of the Agusan River up-stream. Magellan and his men thought the island of Baug was the residence of Rajah Si Ayo. Three days later Magellan would find out that the place was a Royal Hunting Ground, and the thatched structure which Pigafetta described as the king's palace was a hunting lodge, not the king's residence.

Butuan Balangay Boats: Southeast Asian Expedition 2010

Photo Credit: imadylelicer.wordpress.com

CHAPTER V

MAGELLAN IN BAUG ISLAND, MAZZAUA (MADJAWA)

"The most effective way to destroy people is to deny and obliterate their own understanding of their history." – George Orwell

Magellan's Show of Force and Firepower: a Threat

The following morning, Friday, the 29th of March, Good Friday in the Spanish calendar, Magellan sent Enrique, the interpreter, ashore to tell the king of Mazzaua that he wanted to buy some provisions, and that he had come as a friend. Upon hearing this, the king boarded Magellan's ship with eight of his men, bringing raw rice in three porcelain jars, and two big fish, possibly tuna. In return, Magellan gave gifts to the king and his men. After the exchange of gifts, Magellan showed the goods he had on his ship, which included lots of artillery, swords, knives, and shields.

Then, Magellan had some of his artillery fired, which alarmed the king. Magellan also showed off one of his men in metal armor, and had three others strike him with swords and daggers. Pigafetta (68) recorded the king's reaction to this demonstration with the following words: "**Which the king thought very strange**". The Cebuano language translation would be: "*Nagingon ang hari nga lain na man kaayo kini*".

What the king said was actually an understatement expressing alarm. To begin with, Rajah Si Ayo was suspicious of Magellan, and perceived Magellan's show of force as a serious threat. Following the demonstration, Magellan, through his interpreter, told the king of Mazzaua that one metal-armored man in Magellan's ships was worth one hundred of the king's men. Magellan also made the king understand that in each of the three ships were two hundred men like the man in the armor. This was an exaggerated lie. With only three remaining ships out of the five ships that started the voyage in Spain, Magellan had no more than one hundred and fifty men left.

The firing of the artillery, and the display of a lot of weapons, delivered the message that Magellan's fleet had superior firepower and military might. Magellan's declaration about one metal-armored man on his ship being worth one hundred of the king's men only would have compounded Rajah Si Ayo's concern. He understood the whole presentation both as a warning and a grave threat delivered on his own turf by a strange white foreigner who very well could be an invader. Despite the threats, the king of Mazzaua (Madjawa) chose to respond to Magellan's intimidation with peaceful diplomacy. The king must have thought a native armed response would be used only if the situation escalated into a serious crisis, such as an actual armed invasion.

After this, Magellan asked the king if two of his men could go with the king to his residence and to be shown other things in his country. The king agreed. Pigafetta and Enrique went with the king. From Magellan's ship, which was anchored off shore, they took a baloto, a small boat, to the shore.

Pigafetta on Rajah Si Ayo's Balangay Boat

"When I had set foot on shore, the king raised his hand to heaven, then he turned towards us and we did likewise. After this, he took me by the hand, and one of his more notable men took my companion, and he led us to a place covered with reeds, where there was a Ballanghai, that is to say a boat eighty feet or thereabouts in length, like a foist. And there we seated ourselves with the said king on the poop of that boat, always speaking with him by signs" (Pigafetta, 68).

"A place covered with reeds" aptly describes the nipa mangroves that cover the shores of   the small island of Baug (Magallanes) even up to this day. In relation to Pigafetta's description of the king's eighty-foot long boat, it would be interesting to take note of the discovery of an ancient eighty-foot long "Mother Boat" excavated in Butuan in 2012.

Floor of the 80-feet Long Balangay Boat Excavated in Butuan in 2012

While they were on Rajah Si Ayo's balangay boat, Pigafetta took the opportunity to write the names of things in the natives' language.

"And his men stood round us with their swords, spears and buckles. The king then sent for a dish of pork's flesh, and wine. And before the hour of supper I gave the king some things which I had brought. There I wrote down several things as they call them in their language. And when the king and the others saw me writing, and I told them their way of speaking, all were astonished" (Pigafetta, 68).

With regards to Pigafetta's writing of indigenous words, Pigafetta certainly had an excellent ear for languages, and an amazing ability to write native words using phonetic spelling, which in most cases accurately produced the sounds of the words as they were pronounced in the native tongue.

Such talent impressed the natives, and was no doubt an added value to Pigafetta's role as the chronicler of Magellan's voyage.

Native's Use of Porcelain Jars and Dishes

Rice and pork in broth and gravy were served in a large porcelain dish at supper. Pigafetta's accounts on different instances of the native uses of porcelain jars for holding wine and rice, and porcelain dishes for serving food during meals, are consistent with the discovery of hundreds of Chinese porcelain jars, kitchen, house, and dinner wares dating back to the Sung dynasty (10th – 12th centuries A.D.), and the Ming dynasty (14th -15th Centuries A.D.), along with large troves of gold treasures unearthed in Butuan in the early 1970's, and in Surigao in the 1980's.

Ancient Sung and Ming Dynasty Chinese Ceramics Unearthed in Butuan

Pigafetta at the Royal Hunting Lodge

After supper, the king of Mazzaua took them to a structure built with thatch and covered with leaves of fig and palm. Pigafetta used the word *fig* as a substitution for the **banana plant** that does not grow in Europe. The palm refers to the nipa palm leaves from the nipa palm reeds that grow in great abundance around the island. *"It was built up from the ground on thick high posts, and we had to climb up to it by steps and ladders"* (Pigafetta, 69). At first, Pigafetta thought that this was the king's palace, but a couple of days later he would come to know that the place where they were in was a Royal Hunting Ground, and the thatched structure was the Royal Hunting Lodge. A typical native building in the flood plains of the Butuan Delta, the Royal Hunting Lodge was a long house built on thick posts with steps and ladders. The natives usually kept domestic animals on the ground below the wooden or bamboo floors of the building which was constructed at a higher elevation to stay above the water when floods from overflowing rivers came during the rainy monsoon or typhoon season.

At the hunting lodge, the King presented his eldest son, the Prince, to Pigafetta and Enrique. More food was brought in so they could dine with the Prince. Enrique enjoyed himself with so much food and wine that he got intoxicated. They had to spend the night at the hunting lodge.

The next morning, which was a Saturday, Rajah (Si) Ayo came and walked Pigafetta and his companion back to the balangay boat for breakfast, but a skiff from Magellan's ship came to pick them up. At this time, Rajah Kalambu, the king of Butuan, and the brother of Rajah (Si) Ayo, came with three of his men, and went on the boat with them to Magellan's ship. Magellan gave the king of Butuan some gifts, and had him stay for breakfast.

The appearance of the king of Butuan on the second morning after the arrival of Magellan's fleet suggests the close proximity of the palace of the king of Butuan to the Royal Hunting Ground.

Rajah Kalambu, the King of Butuan-Kalagan

The following is Pigafetta's description of Rajah Kalambu: *"And he was the most handsome person whom we saw among those peoples. He had very black hair to his shoulders, with silk cloth on his head, and two large gold rings hanging from his ears. He wore a cotton cloth, embroidered with silk, which covered him from his waist to his knees. At his side he had a dagger, with a long handle, and all of gold, the sheath of which was carved of wood. Withal he wore on his person perfumes of storax and benzoin. He was tawny and painted all over. His island is called Butuan-Calaghan"* (Pigafetta, 69).

Pigafetta's description of Rajah Kalambu as "painted all over", which means the king had tattoos all over his body, is an observation that deserves to be noted for it offers insight into the king's cultural orientation in addition to his status and rank. Lane Wilcken extensively discusses the reasons for the age-old practice of body tattooing among Austronesians, such as the indigenous peoples of the Philippines, and the Pacific islands. Besides the use of tattoos as a preferred body covering in the hot and humid islands, tattoos were expressions of indigenous ancestral spiritual beliefs and cultural values. Tattoos also signified the attainment of exceptional courage. For example, a person could earn new body tattoos with special designs and meanings for each victory in war. Tattoos were also embedded on a person's body to uphold communal and cultural ideals, as well as to preserve the values and memory of their ancestors. If forgotten, ancestral spirits are believed to be capable of unleashing a curse upon the land and its people. (Lane Wilcken, Filipino Tattoos, Ancient to Modern. Schiffer Publishing Ltd. (2010), pp. 66-68).

Rajah Kalambu was a leader who, through his tattoos, wanted to show his faithfulness to ancestral traditions. Moreover, his being tattooed all over indicates that he was a warrior king, and had earned his tattoos for exceptional courage and victory in numerous engagements in warfare, for which Kalagan and Vizzaya warriors were known by several post-Magellan expeditions. Scott (162) wrote that the first three post-Magellan expeditions met hostile reception from the fierce warriors of Kalagan.

It should be noted that Rajah Kalambu was the incumbent king when the Bagani warriors, the indigenous military force of the country, successfully defeated the three post-Magellan Spanish invasions of Butuan-Kalagan.

The Golden Palace of Rajah Kalambu

On the same day, Saturday, March 30, 1521, Pigafetta had a chance to visit and see the palace of the King of Butuan, which at that time was located in Banza (Bangsa), an island in the interior of the Butuan Delta some three miles (approximately seven kilometers) from the confluence of the Agusan River and Butuan Bay. The following is Pigafetta's report of his visit to the palace of the king of Butuan.

"In the island of that king who came to the ship are mines of gold, which are found by digging from the earth large pieces as large as walnuts and eggs. And all the vessels he uses are likewise (of gold) as are also some parts of his house, which was well-fitted in the fashion of the country. And when the two kings wish to visit each other, they go hunting on the island where we were. Of these kings, the aforesaid painted one is named Raia Calambu, and the other Raia Siaiu." (Pigafetta, 69)

Gold Bowl: Surigao Treasures 9th Century, C.E.

Photo credit: nicepicture08.blogspot.com

In Pigafetta's own words he reveals the details of the amazing level of material wealth and culture of the Butuan-Kalagan Gold kingdom. *"Some parts of the king's palace were made of gold, which was well-fitted in the fashion of the country and the king's vessels all of gold, and gold mines"*, eloquently speaks of a kingdom of gold. Pigafetta's words convey that he actually visited the palace of the King of Butuan-Kalagan. The phrase *"which was well-fitted in the fashion of the country"* is a detail that shows Pigafetta making a comparison of the architectural design of the king's palace to other homes or structures that he saw in Butuan. Remnants of an urban center with a thriving gold industry, and large troves of buried gold treasures, were excavated in present-day Butuan City in the mid 1970s.

At this juncture, one might ask why the King of Butuan allowed Pigafetta to see his palace while the King of Mazzaua did his best to hide the location of his residence from Magellan and his men. The palace of the King of Butuan was located in old Banza, an island upstream towards the interior of the Agusan

River, seven kilometers away from Butuan Bay where Magellan's ships with their powerful cannons were anchored. Pigafetta went with Rajah Kalambu on the king's boat to the palace. Pigafetta and Magellan, however, had no idea that it was possible for big ships like Spanish galleons to enter the Agusan River and navigate through it, for it was very deep and remained so until the 1980's. The King of Butuan knew that since Magellan's ships would not go through the Agusan River to the center of the kingdom, there was no chance that Magellan could launch a direct artillery attack against his palace and the city.

The Royal Hunting Ground

On the other hand, the King of Mazzaua had led Magellan's fleet to a hunting ground far away from his residence and government center. The king had been suspicious and distrustful of Magellan since their first face-to-face meeting. Knowing that Magellan's ships were following his balangay boats from Malimono in Surigao, Rajah Si Ayo headed towards Butuan, in the opposite direction to his palace, and stopped at the Royal Hunting Ground, a diversionary tactic designed to hide the exact location of the seat of the kingdom of Mazzaua.

European cartographers made sixteenth and seventeenth century maps that show Mazzaua is in northern Surigao, north of Butuan. The first meeting between Magellan and the King of Mazzaua was on the coastal waters of Malimono in Northern Surigao, based on the navigational coordinates indicated by Pigafetta.

On Easter Sunday, the King of Mazzaua told Magellan that the place where they were was a Royal Hunting Ground where he would go to hunt and see his brother, the King of Butuan. The King of Mazzaua (Madjawa) also explained that his residence and family were on another island. Most likely, Rajah Si Ayo's residence and the seat of the Rajahnate of Mazzaua were located in northern Surigao.

After his first meeting with Magellan offshore in Malimo-no, Rajah Si Ayo suspected that Magellan was an invader. Upon the return of some of his men, who briefly boarded Magellan's ship, Rajah Si Ayo and his men immediately left in their balan-gay boats. Instead of going north towards the seat of his Ra-jahnate in Surigao, to his residence where he lived with his fami-ly and people, Rajah Si Ayo sailed south in the opposite direction towards Butuan. The rajah knew Magellan's ships might follow them. Rajah Si Ayo was right, that was exactly what Magellan's fleet did.

In the evening, Rajah Si Ayo's balangay boats stopped on the shores of an island along Butuan Bay, a safe distance from the palace of his brother, Rajah Kalambu, the King of Butuan-Kalagan. Access to Rajah Kalambu's palace was a good seven kilometers upstream against strong currents towards the interior of the Agusan River, the largest river in Mindanao.

Rajah Si Ayo's decision to stop at the Royal Hunting Ground was a brilliant strategic move to prevent Magellan from getting too close to the epicenter of his kingdom, the Rajahnate of Mazzaua, as well as his brother's kingdom, the Rajahanate of Bu-tuan-Kalagan.

The two brother kings also must have known about the Portuguese incursion into Southeast Asia. The Butuan port had once been a part of the "constellation of stars in the Asia-Pacific Nanhai Trading network" (Hontiveros, 24).They would have known of the Portuguese invasion and conquest of Malacca in the Malay Peninsula just ten years earlier in 1511. They knew Magellan was no accidental tourist, and they were absolutely right about it.

CHAPTER VI

THE FIRST MASS ON PHILIPPINE SOIL

"They came with a Bible and their religion, stole our land, crushed our spirit....and now tell us we should be thankful to the 'Lord' for being saved." – Chief Pontiac (d. 1769).

Planting Christianity in the Land of Aba (Abba)

It was Easter Sunday, March 31, 1521, the day after Pigafetta's visit to the palace of the King of Butuan. Pigafetta's eyewitness report of the king's golden palace, his gold vessels, and the gold mines that were the source of the gold, strongly confirmed to Magellan that he had reached the gold islands. The confirmation activated Magellan's conquistador instincts, and put in motion his secret agenda: to take control of the islands of gold. He needed to take immediate action.

God, Gold and Glory, the mantra of the European Age of Discovery, appeared to have worked in Magellan's favor. With the priest Valderama and fifty of his men, Magellan went ashore and held mass to celebrate the great discovery of the gold islands on Easter Sunday.

In actual application and practice, the Spaniards and the Portuguese used God, the Roman Catholic religion, and military force to acquire gold and take possession and control of "discovered lands". The Spaniards and the Portuguese, the leading 16th century colonizers, believed that with the Pope's blessings, and the mandate of the Emperor of the Holy Roman Empire, they were entitled to claim lands, and take all the gold they could get their hands on, outside of Europe. They embarked on this mission with the help of the cross, and especially, the sword. A soldier and explorer, Magellan himself possessed both the experience and the orientation to act on opportunities for gold, glory, and territorial expansion.

Maps showing Magallanes (Baug)

The Mass in Baug, Mazzaua

Magellan and 50 of his men celebrated the first mass on Philippine soil in Baug, the Royal Hunting Ground, on Easter Sunday, March 31, 1521. Baug was one of the islands that belonged to the Rajahnate of Mazzaua, on the western coastline of Northern Mindanao. According to the oral tradition of the people of Baug, the first mass was held there, in an area which became the Butuan town center in 1868. The Spanish authorities relocated the government center from its former location in Banza to Baug. The people who moved to the relocation site insisted on retaining the name Butuan to refer to Baug, the new town center.

In 1872, Jose Maria Carvallo, the then-Governor of the Surigao-Butuan Spanish colonial territories, put up a stone marker in Baug, declaring the place the site of the first mass. In 1877, the Butuan town center in Baug was again transferred to the island of Agao in the Butuan Delta, where it has remained until today (Hontiveros, 149). Baug is now called Magallanes. The First Mass stone marker still stands today on the shore of Magallanes.

Discovery of Mindanao Gold:

The Real Significance of Magellan's First Mass

Besides the fact that it was Easter Sunday, the real significance of the mass in Baug was the celebration of Magellan's discovery of the gold islands, his intended secret destination.

The following is Pigafetta's account of the first mass: "*On Sunday, the last day of March, and Easter Day, the captain early in the morning sent the Chaplain ashore to celebrate mass. And the interpreter went with him to tell the king that we were not landing to dine with him, but only to hear mass. Hearing this, the king sent two dead pigs. And when the hour for hearing mass came, the captain with fifty men went ashore, not in armor, but only with swords, and dressed as honorably as possible for each man to do. And before we reached shore with the boats, our ships fired six shots as a sign of peace. When we landed, the two kings were there, and they received our king kindly, and put him in the center between the two of them. Then we went to the place prepared for saying mass which was not far from the shore.*" (Pigafetta, 70)

After mass, Magellan, through the interpreter, asked the two kings several questions. First, Magellan wanted to know if the kings were heathen or Moor (Muslim). The two kings answered that they worshipped Aba, an Indo-Aryan word, meaning father. In the context of the conversation, this would mean God the Father. The two kings were not Moors (Muslims). This Indo-Aryan religious element would just have been a layer over the Austronesian Animist spiritual core beliefs of the natives.

At least five hundred years before the coming of Magellan to the kingdoms of Mazzaua and Butuan-Kalagan, the influence of the Buddhist culture of the great and powerful Sri Vijaya Empire, seated in Palembang Sumatra (7th -13th century AD), the world's longest-running empire, and later the Hindu Madjapahit Empire in Java (1293 -1500 AD) had already spread and taken root in Southeast Asia, including the pre-Philippine islands. In fact, the Vijaya Islands in the central part of the

Archipelago earned such a name in reference to the many groups of peoples who speak the Vijaya languages and trace their origins to the Sri Vijaya Empire in Sumatra. Sri Vijaya is Sankskrit, an ancient classical Indo-Aryan language. Sri means "shining" or "radiant", and Vijaya means "excellence" or victory". The word Ka-Vijayaan or Ka-Bisayaan refers to the Vijaya islands and the people of the Vizzaya islands and Mindanao who speak languages classifed as Vijaya/Vizzaya. The word "Aba" has its origins in the Hindu-Buddhist culture of both the Sri Vijaya and Madjapahit empires.

Today "Aba" is spoken in Tagalog at the beginning of a sentence to express surprise, or with an emphasis equivalent to "Oh God" in English. "Aba" is also part of the opening sentence of the Hail Mary addressed to Mary, the Mother of Jesus. It goes this way: "Aba Ginoong Maria..." Some Filipino family names start with "Aba" such as Abalos, Abarquez, Abarientos, and Abad, to name a few.

"Aba" is also part of **Abadeha**, the name of the Philippine Cinderella. Abadeha is an indigenous Cinderella fairy tale that originated from the Vizzaya Region, most likely from the country of Butuan-Kalagan. "Aba" is God and "deha/diha" means land in Sankskrit. **Abadeha** would mean "land of God". In Persia (Iran) there is an ancient city called Abadeh.

It was also after mass that Magellan asked why there was very little food on the "place where they were". Magellan must have noticed the absence of a settled community on the island, thus the scarcity of provisions. The following is Rajah Si Ayo's response, *"The king replied that he did not sojourn in that place except when he went hunting, or to see his brother, but that he lived on another island, where he had all his family."*

(Pigafetta, 71).

Rajah si Ayo says that he would come to this place only to hunt or meet his brother, Rajah Kalambu, the king of Butuan, and that Rajah Si Ayo's residence or palace was on another island where his family also resided. Rajah Si Ayo's explanation further confirms the close proximity of the Royal Hunting Ground to the residence of the King of Butuan, which Pigafetta visited the day before. It is also clear that Magellan's fleet followed Rajah Si Ayo's Balangay boats from Malimono, "the latitude of nine and two thirds degrees toward the Arctic Pole, and in the longitude of one hundred and sixty two from the line of demarcation" (Pigafetta, 72). The king deliberately stopped at the mostly uninhabited Royal Hunting Ground, instead of going to the seat of his kingdom. Rajah Si Ayo needed to prevent Magellan's fleet from getting to the center of the kingdom of Mazzaua for security reasons. From the start, he suspected that Magellan was an invader. It would be foolhardy to lead an invader to the seat of his territory, to the port and government center of his rajahnate, to his home, the residence of his family and the majority of his people.

Magellan also asked Rajah Si Ayo if he had enemies who made war with him. If he had any, Magellan offered to go with his men and ships to attack and subjugate them. Regarding this, Pigafetta wrote the following: "Then the captain caused him to be asked whether he had enemies who made war on him, for if he had any, he would go with his men and ships to destroy them into submission to him. The king in reply said that there were two islands whose people were his enemies, but that this was not the season at which to go and attack them."

(Pigafetta, 71).

Rajah Si Ayo's response showed diplomatic and political sophistication. He understood that Magellan was playing the proverbial "Divide and Conquer Game". The king knew better than to take Magellan's bait. Rajah Si Ayo was well aware that allowing a stranger and foreigner to go to war against one's enemies was tantamount to surrendering his authority and control over his territory and political affairs to that person. Rajah Si Ayo, and his brother Rajah Kalambu, understood fully well Magellan's game. They were not stupid. Magellan's offer also conveyed an implied intention to stay and take control. The real and present danger of Magellan's plan would have seriously alarmed the two brother kings.

Since Magellan already had the confirmation that they had come upon the kingdoms of gold, Magellan wanted to act fast. The two kings would have been concerned, but were quite good at hiding their true feelings, thoughts, and reactions to avoid a potentially catastrophic and bloody frontal war. They realized that they would have to fight an enemy with superior arms and firepower should war erupt between them and Magellan.

Staking the Spanish Claim with the Cross

After dinner, both kings went with Magellan, some of his men, the interpreter, and Pigafetta to the highest mountain nearby to plant a cross on its peak. Pigafetta narrates how Magellan explained the necessity of planting the cross: *"And he told them that he wished to set them upon their country for their benefit, so that if any ships of Spain came afterward to those islands, they seeing the said cross would know that we had been there. And by this token they would do them no harm, and if they took any of their men, being immediately shown this sign, they would*

let them go. Moreover, the captain told them that it was neces-
sary that the cross be set up at the top of the highest mountain
in their country, so that everyday seeing the said cross, they
might worship it, and that if they did this, not thunder, light-
ning, nor tempest could harm them." (Pigafetta, 70).

Magellan explained that the cross would protect the natives from harm, and if other Spanish ships would come, they
would not harm the natives if they saw the cross. This, of course,
was another big lie, and the two brother kings knew it. They fully understood Magellan's game of deception, and they realized
they had to play their part in the game.

By planting the cross on the mountain, Magellan had
staked his claim on the gold kingdoms, securing them for the
Spanish Empire. Finding this land of gold was literally hitting
the mother lode of the voyage. After enduring and surviving the
terrible perils, hardships, disease, starvation and loss of many
lives on the seas from Spain, to South America, then across the
Pacific, discovering these gold kingdoms must have been the ultimate reward. Taking ownership of these gold islands was a bo-
nanza too valuable to pass up. Magellan needed to grab the lit-
eral golden opportunity of a lifetime which was now at hand.
Finding these gold islands was, after all, Magellan's hidden personal purpose for going on the voyage. In the face of this incredi-
ble discovery, Magellan's decision to stay and conquer the gold
kingdoms would be wise and sensible, but it was doomed to fail.

Magellan Starts Move to Conquer the Gold Islands

After the cross was erected, Magellan wanted to know the
location of the best trading port. The two kings informed him
that the good trading ports were in Ceylon, (Leyte), Kalagan and
Zzubu (Sugbo/Cebu), and the best was Cebu. Based on Magellan's question regarding the location of the best port, the two native brother kings knew what Magellan wanted to do.

Once Magellan had staked his claim, the next move was to go to Cebu, the richest and biggest trading port, then take control of it. After securing the Port of Cebu, he would then take the port kingdoms of Butuan, Mazzaua, and Ceylon (Leyte), in effect taking control of the trade network of the gold islands with the other countries in the Asia-Pacific region. Magellan knew that taking control of the trading centers was a successful strategy for conquest, proven by the Portuguese in Malacca in 1511.

Now that Magellan had found the strait that connected to the great Pacific Ocean, a westward route to Southeast Asia, the best trading port on these islands of gold could become the Spanish-controlled center of trade between Asia and Europe, providing a strong competition to the Portuguese controlled port of Malacca. Rich in natural resources and abundant deposits and supplies of gold, these islands would have much to offer in trade, and could generate great wealth and glory for the Spanish empire, and Magellan himself.

The two brother kings, the rajahs of the two richest and most powerful rajanates of Butuan and Mazzaua in Northern Mindanao, fully understood Magellan's intentions, and the urgent necessity to act in defense of their kingdoms. They knew it was critically necessary to stop Magellan, and get rid of him.

Magellan wanted to immediately leave for Cebu the next day, and asked the kings to provide him with guides to get there. Magellan promised to treat the guides well, and offered to leave one of his men as collateral. The two kings initially agreed to Magellan's request, although the urgency of Magellan's desire to get to Cebu would only have confirmed the two king's assessment of his intent to immediately take control of the port.

CHAPTER VII

THE BEGINNING OF THE NATIVE CONSPIRACY

" When the evidence changes, the history books need to be rewritten."

– Sam Winburg, History Author/Professor, Stanford University

Rajah Si Ayo Changes His Mind

On the morning of the next day, Monday, when Magellan and his men were ready to sail for Cebu, Rajah Si Ayo informed them that he had changed his mind. He, the king himself, would guide Magellan's fleet to Cebu, but he needed two days to have his rice harvested. He also added that he had other things to do, and asked Magellan to lend him some men to help with the work of harvesting the rice so that they could finish the work sooner.

That day the two kings supposedly ate and drank so much wine that they fell asleep and nothing was done: *"But the kings ate and drank so much that they slept all day. And some to excuse them, said that they were sick. Wherefore we did nothing that day. But the two days following we labored"* (Pigafetta, 71-72).

Delaying Tactics of the Two Kings

The new developments coming from the two brother kings marked the beginning of the native conspiracy against Magellan. Rajah Si Ayo's change of mind and offer to guide Magellan to Cebu, having Magellan's men help with the rice harvest for two days, and the supposed intoxication and/or illness of the two kings were all delaying tactics designed to postpone Magellan's trip to Cebu.

The delay of three days from the originally planned departure time from Baug, plus another three days of sailing time to Cebu, provided sufficient time for the two brother kings to send an advance party to warn their relative, Rajah Humabon (Umabong), the King of Cebu, of a possible invasion from Magellan's fleet. Rajah Si Ayo himself offered to guide Magellan to Cebu. These actions of Rajah Si Ayo were strategies that would later continue and develop into a clever conspiracy in Cebu. Rajah Si Ayo, Rajah Humabon of Cebu, and his chief men would be involved in the plot of a conspiracy against Magellan. Although Rajah Si Ayo still maintained a friendly and cooperative attitude towards Magellan, he had an ulterior motive in going with Magellan to Cebu. He wanted to personally meet and speak with Rajah Humabon, to secretly plan the conspiracy.

The origin of the conspiracy in Baug on Butuan Bay is not mentioned in Pigafetta's book, but the details of the series of events, and the actions of both Magellan and the two kings in Baug, as well as the 'undercover' role that Rajah Si Ayo played in Cebu would confirm the beginnings of the conspiracy.

Magellan Maintains a Disguised Stance Regarding the Natives' Gold

During the days of the rice harvest, a native offered to trade a crown of massy gold with Magellan's men. Pigafetta noted Magellan's position regarding gold transactions with the natives in the following account:

"Not long after, one of our men went ashore to fetch water, and one of the people aforesaid wished to give him a pointed crown of massy gold for six large pieces of glass. But the captain would not allow such exchange to be made, in order that those people should know that we prized and held in more regard our merchandise than their gold" (Pigafetta, 72). Here again, Magellan declined the gold transaction to deceive the natives into thinking that their gold was not much of value, showing the same attitude when he refused to accept the bar of gold during his first meeting with Rajah Si Ayo. Behind Magellan's consistent display of disinterest in the natives' gold was an ulterior motive. Beneath the façade of dismissing the natives' gold as not valuable, Magellan concealed his true intent, which was to take ownership not just of a few pieces of gold, but of the islands of gold.

The Rajahnate of Mazzaua

Based on pieces of information that Pigafetta wrote, the Rajahnate of Mazzaua was a large territory that spanned from the Dinagat Islands in northern Surigao, stretching south on the western coast of Mindanao, to northern Agusan down to Misamis ending to the immediate north of Quippit on Sindangan Bay in northern Zamboanga. Big and tall mountain ranges such as the Hilong-Hilong and Diwata Mountains serve as the natural boundaries between the Rajahnate of Mazzaua on the northwest coast, and the Rajahnate of Butuan-Kalagan on the northeast coast facing the Pacific Ocean. The Rajahnate of Mazzaua was more or less the other half of the country of Kalagan.

The Rajahnate of Mazzaua was ruled by a king who was also a rajah. The title rajah was used to refer only to a paramount ruler who controlled a port engaged in foreign trade (Scott, 128, 220). Since Si Ayo was the Rajah of Mazzaua, this means Mazzaua had its own port with foreign trade transactions. The location of this port must have been in Northern Surigao in today's Surigao City.

The Natives of the Mazzaua Rice Farming Village in Baug

During the days of the rice harvest, Pigafetta had a chance to see the people in the rice farm in Baug. *"Those people are heathens, and go naked, and are painted, and wear a piece of cloth made from a tree like linen round their private parts, and they are great drinkers. The women are clad in tree cloth from the waist down. And they have black hair hanging down to the ground, and they wear certain gold rings in their ears. Those people chew most of the time a fruit they call Areca, which is something like a pear, and they cut it into quarters, then wrap it in leaves of its tree, called Betre, and they are like mulberry leaves. And mixing it with a little lime, after they have chewed it for a very long time, they spit and throw it out. And from this they afterward have a very red mouth. And many people use the said*
81

fruit because it greatly refreshes them, for the country is so hot that they could not live without it" (Pigafetta, 72).

The Natural Resources of Mazzaua (Madjawa)

"In that island there is a great quantity of dogs, cats, pigs, poultry, and goats, of rice, ginger, coconuts, figs, oranges, lemons, millet, wax, and gold mines" (Pigafetta, 72). The words 'great quantity' describes the abundance of domestic and farm animals as well as farm products, especially rice and coconuts, in that part of Mazzaua (Madjawa). The island is Baug (present-day Magallanes), and its villages along the coast of Butuan Bay which were once part of the Rajahnate of Mazzaua (Madjawa). Among the raw materials mentioned is beeswax from the virgin forests. Wax is an essential material in fashioning raw gold into ornaments, and was traded as an export product along with the gold ornaments and gold ore from Mazzaua. Above all, Pigafetta describes Mazzaua as a land of gold mines, an outstanding feature of northern Mindanao. During Pigafetta's visit to the Golden Palace of the King of Butuan-Kalagan he must have also learned about the goldmines in Mazzaua, which was the other kingdom and rajahnate of the country of Butuan-Kalagan.

Mazzaua in Old Maps

Old European maps show Mazzaua in Surigao north of Butuan in Northern Mindanao. In 1570, Abraham Ortelius, the official cartographer of King Phillip II, constructed a map showing Mazzaua, spelled "Mejsana", in Northern Mindanao. In 1595, European map-maker Gerard Mercator drew a map with Mazzaua, spelled "Malagua", also shown in Surigao. Jodocus Hondius, in 1640, made a map of Mindanao placing Mazzaua, spelled "Malagua", in Northern Mindanao north of Surigao, spelled "Surica" on the map (Gabriel Atega, Mazzawa and The Celebrations of the First Holy Week, Midtown Printing Co. Inc. (2007), pp. 119, 120). The navigational logs of Francisco Albo, the pilot of Magellan's ship, and Judicibus from Genoa, place the location of Mazzaua in northeastern Mindanao (Gabriel Atega, pp. 60-61).

The Rajahnate of Mazzaua included in its territory many islands. Pigafetta (75) refers to Rajah Si Ayo as 'Lord of many islands', adding to his description of the territorial domain of Mazzaua. The 'many islands' probably refers to the Dinagat Islands in Surigao del Norte, as well as all other islands, big and small, within the territory of Mazzaua.

Mazzaua, however, was not confined to northeastern Mindanao. After fleeing from Cebu, the Magellan survivors sailed back to Mindanao and landed in Quippit in Northern Zamboanga, on the border of Misamis, which was still part of Mazzaua. Pigafetta wrote (75) that Quippit borders Mazzaua, and is on the same land as Butuan-Kalagan.

The Butuan Rajahnate

Following the river tributaries from the southern part of East Mindanao, some Manobo people took their balangay boats on the Agusan River that runs across the middle of the island of Mindanao, from the southeastern highlands facing the Pacific Ocean down to the north side, facing Butuan Bay. The Agusan River branches down to the flood plains of Butuan City, forming the islands in the Butuan Delta near the mouth of the river as it joins Butuan Bay.

When the Manobo arrived in Butuan, the Mamanwa and Aeta, the black-skinned proto-Austronesians, and aboriginal inhabitants of the pre-Philippine islands, were already there. Shell middens with bottom layers that started 7000 years ago discovered in recent years in the community of Libertad, provide evidence that black proto-Austronesians were the original inhabitants of Butuan.

The Manobo who later came to Butuan established settlements and lived with the Mamanwa and Aeta in the Butuan Delta. These island settlements became the Rajahnate of Butuan. Nomadic sea merchants, boat-builders, and fishermen, the Sama from Zamboanga arrived in Butuan and took sanctuary in the

Butuan Delta around 800 A.D. This group of Sama men married Manobo women in Butuan and had families with them. The coming together of the Sama men and Manobo women produced the Butuanon people and language. (Margarita Cembrano, Patterns of the Past: The Ethno Archaelogy of Butuan, The National Museum of the Philippines (1998), p.22).

Based on historical and archaelogical evidence, the ancient Butuan Port was the major trading center of the pre-Philippine islands from the 9th- 12th centuries A.D. It was part of the Chinese Nanhai South Sea trading network and the Sri Vijaya trade route in Southeast Asia. The Nanhai trading network came from China, and included Japan, Cambodia, Burma, Vietnam, Thailand, Indonesia, the Malay Peninsula, India, Persia and Arabia (Hontiveros, 40, 41).

The Sri Vijaya was a maritime empire (7th -13th centuries AD) that controlled and managed the sea lanes and the goods traded at the ports of the Southeast Asian states and countries in the network. "The Srivijaya (at its peak in the ninth century AD and its final decline in the 14th century AD) was a maritime empire, whose dependencies were basically commercial outposts and entrepots, centers which stimulated trade in the regions along the periphery of their direct control. Historically, long distance trading enterprises in insular southeast Asia required strategic points on the trading circuits posts which provided security and facilities for repair and re-supply" (Cembrano, 26).

Butuan succeeded through its own initiative in consolidating the different islands, and the coastal and in-land communities in the southern Philippines in their participation in the Sri Vijaya trading network, stimulating the dynamic production and exchange of marketable goods and economic growth in the Vizzaya culture region of the Mindanao and Vizzayas. More diplomatic and trade alliances with China and other kingdoms were forged during the Golden Age of the Sri Vijaya Empire (Cembrano, 26). The trade collaboration of the Sri Vijaya trading and Nanhai trading networks was established and lasted several centuries during the existence of the Sri Vijaya Empire.

The kingdom of Butuan included in its territory all the districts and villages in Butuan City, the villages towards southern Agusan, along the Agusan River towards the mountains up to the Pacific coast, Bislig Island, and all the islands of southern Surigao on the eastern Pacific.

Butuan-Kalagan: Ancient Country in the pre-Philippine Islands

When Magellan's voyage reached Mindanao, he had visited the country of Butuan-Kalagan, and parts of its two rajahnates, the Rajahnate of Mazzaua, and the Rajahnate of Butuan. Pigafetta referred to Rajah Kalambu as the King of Butuan-Kalagan, not just Butuan. This means Rajah Kalambu was the king of the Rajahnate of Butuan and also the ruler of the whole country of Kalagan. Ancient Kalagan was a country with two kingdoms which were also rajahnates, since these kingdoms had ports which were engaged in foreign trade. The two rajahnates were the Rajahnate of Butuan and the Rajahnate of Mazzaua (Madjawa). The country of Butuan-Kalagan included the city of Butuan and all its villages, all of southern and northern Agusan, southern and northern Surigao, northern Davao and Misamis. *Caraga Antigua*, a book by Peter Schreuers, published in 1989, includes all of Agusan, Surigao, and Davao (except Misamis) in its definition.

The existence and primacy of the country of Butuan-Kalagan predates all other rajahnates and sultanates of the pre-Philippine islands. Only Butuan-Kalagan, and no other place within the archipelago, has a historical existence recorded in ancient Chinese annals dating back one thousand years ago, and five hundred years before the coming of the Europeans to the islands.

The Chinese **Song Shih** (Song History) is the earliest source of the ethno-history of Butuan, referred to as "(**P'u-tuan**) a **small country in the sea** that had regular dealings with Champa, a small kingdom in central Vietnam, and intermittent contact with China." (Cembrano, 25). Butuan indirectly traded with China through Vietnam for some time. China identified the small country as Butuan because the international trading port and capital of the country was in Butuan. It should also be noted that in response to Magellan's inquiry about the best ports in the islands, the two kings mentioned three ports: Ceylon (Leyte), Cebu and Calaghan (Kalagan). The kings referred to the port in Butuan as Kalagan, meaning the Butuan port was the major port of the country of Kalagan.

Butuan-Kalagan in the year 1001 A.D. was the first country-state within the pre-Philippine archipelago to send a tributary mission to China. Following three other trade missions from Butuan, on March 1011, China approved direct diplomatic and trade relations with Butuan-Kalagan (Cembrano, 25). The establishment of direct ties with China, the Asian superpower of that time, implies that Butuan-Kalagan was a stable, civilized country. China gave the Butuan envoy, General Li-Gan-Xie, sent by Rajah Sri Bata Shaja the title 'Gently Reconciling General'. (Hontiveros, 39). The name Li-Gan-Xie is the Chinese version of Sri Li-Gan. Today, people with the family name Ligan still live in the neighboring cities of Cabadbaran and Butuan.

The hundreds of Chinese ceramics, jars, bowls and gold ornaments excavated in the environs of the Butuan Delta tell the compelling story of the long-standing trade relations in ancient times between Butuan-Kalagan and China, dating back from the Sung Dynasty to the Ming Dynasty, a period of approximately five hundred years.

The pre-colonial country of Butuan-Kalagan in northern Mindanao, with its capital and trading port in Butuan City, was the center of indigenous Austronesian-Malay socio- economic, political and cultural power in the pre-Philippines for at least four centuries, from the 9th-13th centuries AD. In addition to ancient Chinese historical records, archaeological evidence, such as gold treasures, a fleet of ancient boats, and other artifacts, excavated in Butuan and Surigao, establish the existence of the rich and ancient country of Butuan-Kalagan, and its age-old

Austronesian classical culture.

The Butuan-Kalagan Gold Country

The Butuan-Kalagan kingdom was known as the wealthiest in Mindanao, if not all of the Philippine islands (Hontiveros, 78). Besides the fact that it was rich in agriculture, forest products, and had an amazing diversity of marine life, the kingdom was the most abundant source of gold. Unearthed in the 1970s and 80s in Butuan City and Surigao del Sur, places within the domain of the ancient Butuan-Kalagan kingdom, were large troves of stunning, elaborate ancient gold treasures, with ceramic jars dating back to the 9th century AD. The construction of new roads, fish ponds, and flood control canals in Butuan in the mid-seventies inadvertently yielded large volumes of buried gold treasures triggering the 'Butuan Gold Rush'. Following the gold treasure discoveries, treasure hunters and gold-seekers literally started digging for buried gold in the old Butuan districts of Masao and Libertad.

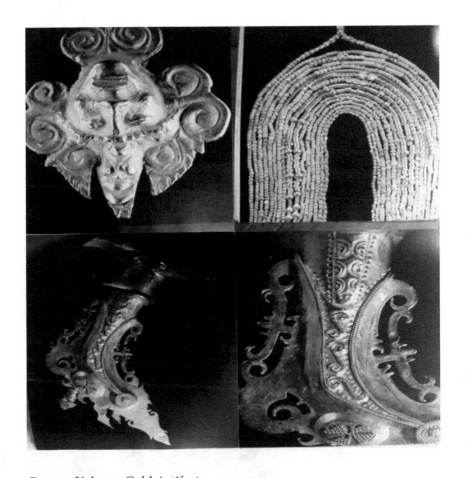

Butuan-Kalagan Gold Artifacts

Photo Credit: Central Bank of the Philippines

A significant number of stunning gold artifacts (including jewelry, funerary masks, diadems, royal belts, purses, receptacles, baskets, figurines, and even chastity covers) from unusually large troves of gold treasures accidentally excavated in Surigao and Butuan in northeastern Mindanao, are now at the Ayala Museum in Makati City, where an impressive and stunning gold collection of 1,100 gold artifacts are on exhibit. Several hundred more gold artifacts are among the Surigao Gold Treasures Exhibit at the Manila Metropolitan Museum in the Central Bank of the Philippines. An undetermined number of gold artifacts remain in the private collections of individuals, some of whom are in

Butuan City and Manila.

Many of the gold treasures discovered in Butuan came from the ancient graves of both native royalty and commoners. Other gold treasures were buried on hillsides and swamp grounds, an indication that the natives tried to hide their gold treasures from the hands of gold-greedy Spanish colonizers who came and conquered the pre-Philippines from 1565 onwards.

Butuan-Kalagan Gold Artifacts

Photo Credit: Central Bank of the Philippines

Gold ornaments and Chinese ceramics from the Song Dynasty were also excavated in the nearby coastal communities and former pre-colonial trading satellites of La Union, in Kaasinan in Cabadbaran, in Manapa, and in Abilan in the municipality of Buenavista in northern Agusan (Cembrano, 33).

Traders from within the pre-Philippine archipelago Hawa (Java), Borneo, Moluccas, Malacca, Sumatra, Thailand, Vietnam, China, Japan, India, Persia and Arabia came for Butuan's gold, civet cats, and beeswax, a necessary material for fashioning gold ornaments and jewelry.

The People of Butuan-Kalagan

A better understanding of the historical significance of Butuan-Kalagan, and its influence in the development of the pre-Philippines, starts with a knowledge of the origins and history of the Austronesian people who established, more than a thousand years ago, the first and only sovereign country within the Philippine archipelago.

The Manobo people were the ethnic majority in ancient Kalagan. Proto-Manobo speakers arrived in East Mindanao on the Pacific coast around 500 C.E. (Cembrano, 21). They were among the many groups of Austronesian-Malays from Southern China who migrated back to their Austronesian homeland in the Southeast Asian Islands (Jesus Peralta, The Austronesian Expansion – A Reaction to Paths of Origin, Manila, Philippines, National Commission for Culture and the Arts, (2011).

Manobo (Lumad) People in Caraga

Photo Credit: *onebillionrising.org*

Kulintang Musicians

Photo Credit: trekearth.com

Ancient artifacts found in Butuan City in the last four decades show Austronesian origins from Southern China. The Austro-Asiatic people (black Asians) started their dispersal from Sundaland (the pre-deluvian Southeast Asian Continent) around 7,000 years ago during the floods that drowned most of the lowlands of Sundaland. Many of them ended up in coastal areas of Southern China (Stephen Oppenheimer, Eden in the East: The Drowned Continent of Southeast Asia, (1998) pp. 50, 78). In Kalagan, the Manobo came to live with the Mamanwa and the Aeta, the proto-Austronesians or black-skinned aborigines who stayed behind or were stranded during the flooding of Sundaland.

The term **Manobo** is derived from man and **obo** or **ubu**. **Man** means person or people; **obo** or **ubu** means originally grown or native. **Manobo**, therefore, means indigenous people. The affix **man** or **mang** precedes occupation, activity or location in numerous Filipino noun words. A few examples are the following: **mandaragat** (man or people who navigate), **manlulupig** (man or people who subjugate others), **mandirigma** (man or people who fight in war), **manananggot** (man or people who gather wine from the coconut tree), **mandarambong** (man or people who engage in plunder), **manlilinlang** (man or people who deceive others), **manggagamot** (man or people who practice medicine), **mananahi** (man or people who engage in sewing), **manlilikha** (man or people who create), and **manggagawa** (man or people who engage in manual labor).

The Manobo in Agusan, Surigao, Davao and Misamis include many sub-groups such as the Butuanon in Butuan, the Kamayo in Surigao, the Tagkaolo (also called Kalagan) in Surigao and Davao, the Mansaka, the Mandaya, and the Bagobo in Davao, the Banwaon, the Ata Manobo, the Matigsalug Manobo, the Dalangan Manobo and the Ubu.

The Sama People in Butuan-Kalagan

Around 800 A.D. a group of **Sama** men came to Butuan, and took sanctuary in the Butuan Delta. Expert boat builders, divers, advanced navigators and fishermen, the Sama also were nomadic sea merchants (Cembrano, 27). They first appeared in Zamboanga in southern Mindanao. "The origin of the word Sama was traced in the ancient Chinese annal called San-Hai-Ching (Mountain - sea book) written in ca. 2205–100 B.C. The Sama were described as a united people who rose in rebellion against the Shun ruler, and thereafter fled to the South Seas where the country of the Sam-ma was established" (Cembrano, 19).

The Sama country appears to be the Austronesian homeland in the islands of Sulawesi in eastern Indonesia, and the southern Philippines, which is "the center of innovation of all Austronesian boat traits" (Oppenheimer, 65). The Sama men married local Manobo women in Butuan. The coming together of Sama men and the Manobo women in Butuan produced the Butuanon people and language.

Sama Girls in Traditional Clothing

Photo Credit: CEphoto

Sama Lepa Boat c.1903

Photo Credit: David P. Barrows (1905)

A Regatta Lepa Festival in Semporna, Borneo

Photo Credit: CEphoto, Uwe Aranas

Around 1300 A.D. a large group of Butuanon people made a mass migration to Jolo in the central part of Sulu Islands. They became known as the Tausug. The Tausug people of Sulu and the Butuanon people, therefore, are related by both language and blood (Cembrano, 22).

The Sama-Manobo men from Butuan who went on fishing trips in the Hinatuan Passage in the Pacific Ocean east of Butuan-Kalagan also took wives among the Manobo coastal communities, producing the Kamayo people and language.

The people of Butuan-Kalagan were collectively called **Vizzaya.** *"It was on the Pacific coast in what is now Surigao del Sur, and Davao Oriental that Spaniards first learned the name 'Vizaya.' Dutch records also refer to southeastern Mindanao, as Bisaya, and Villalobos in 1543 called Davao Gulf, Bisaya Bay"* (Scott, 162).

It appears the word **Vizzaya/Bisaya** refers to the people who spoke the Vizzaya languages in Mindanao, and the Vizzayas, and must have been identified as such in association with the inclusion of the Philippines as a part of the Sri Vijaya Empire (700 – 1300 A.D.). Even Tagalog, the language of Manila, and most of Luzon is classified as originally a central Vizzaya language. Cebuano is the major Vizzaya language that is spoken and understood in the Vizzaya cultural region of Mindanao and the Vizzayan islands.

The name **kalagan** is derived from the Vizzaya word **kalag,** meaning **soul** or **spirit. The suffix 'an' which joins kalag at the end means 'the state of being' or 'the place, territory or domain. Kalagan,** therefore, means **a spiritual place.** In Tagalog, **kalagan** means **to set free.** Combined with the Vijaya meaning of the word, **kalagan,** would mean **land of free souls. Vizzaya people** call violent people **"mga two nga walay kalag"**, people without souls.

'Kalagan' could also be the natives' **metaphor for gold, the metal of the gods.** Kalagan in this regard might also be interpreted as **the land of gold.** The natives believe in **Animism,** the concept that all creation, both living and non-living, has a life force or soul which like gold is supremely radiant and indestructible.

The Sama-Manobo-Bisaya Expansion and Influence

The Sama-Manobo people engaged in fishing, trading, and boat-building activities not just around the Mindanao coastal areas. Their migratory lifestyle connected to sailing in the oceans and seas also took them to the Vizzaya islands, and Luzon. Their communally organized fishing expeditions in fleets of boats, with oarsmen and expert harpooners, took them to their favorite traditional fishing grounds in the high seas in the San Bernardino Pass between Capul Island and Northern Samar, the Davao Gulf, and Hinatuan Passage in northeast Mindanao, northern Luzon as far as the the Batanes Islands, and even Taiwan (Cembrano, 27). The Sama-Manobo spread not only their fishing, boat-building, pottery-making, and trading skills and traditions, but also the Bisaya languages and culture along the coastal regions of Luzon. "Visayan culture and languages are the most widely dispersed in the archipelago" (Scott, 4). This could explain the classification of Tagalog as a central Vizzaya language. When Sultan Bulkeiah of Borneo conquered Manila and Luzon in 1500 A.D., the language of the region changed with the infusion of Bornean. This has now become the contemporary Tagalog language. "Tagalog has more Malay loan words than any other major Philippine languages" (Scott, 9). The Tagalog word **kasama** means **fellow-Sama**. The following are a few examples of language cognates based on Vizzaya vocabulary words.

Butuanon- Sama-Manobo-Cebuano-Tagalog Cognates

gunting	scissors
sanduk	ladle
sulo	torchlight
palay/paray	unhusked rice
bigas/bugas	polished rice
saging	banana
manga	mango
kamanyang	resins
hayup	domesticated animals
bihag	losing a cock in a cockfight
banig	mat
luto	to cook
sanglag/sangag	to toast in a pan
bogay/bagay	communal sharing
handog (Banwaon, Tagalog)	offering
tapa	dried meat
laksoy	nipa wine
baboy	pig
manok	chicken
kanin/kanon	boiled rice
tubig	water
hangin	air, wind
dagat	sea
lawod/laut	ocean

Butuanon- Sama-Manobo Cebuano-Tagalog Cognates

balay/bahay	house
ngipin/ngipon	teeth
tainga/talinga	ear
ilong	nose
mata	eyes
ulipon/alipin	slave
layag	sail
langoy	swim
luha	tears
halok/halik	kiss
hapon	afternoon
gabii/gabi	night
bulan/buwan	moon
bituon/bituin	star
langit	sky/heaven

Magellan Sails to Cebu

Ignorant of the age-old socio-political-economic connections of the Northeastern Mindanao rajanates with the Rajanate of Cebu, Magellan simply headed for Cebu with conquest on his mind. As I have explained, at the time of Magellan's coming, the kingdoms of Mazzaua, Butuan-Kalagan, Cebu, and the other kingdoms of the islands, were thriving societies with long-established socio-economic-political and cultural systems, traditions, and alliances. The country of Butuan-Kalagan had cultural and trading ties with its Southeast Asian neighbors, China, India, and the Middle East that had been long-established and had flourished for at least five hundred years before the coming of the Europeans.

In the face of the reality that he had reached the gold islands, the secret destination of his voyage, Magellan refused to consider the increased odds of conquering the islands. When the voyage reached the pre-Philippine islands, his fleet had only three ships left of the original five, and more or less 150 of the 240 men he had when they left Spain. Despite the diminished resources and number of men, Magellan obstinately decided to go ahead with his hidden agenda. Lacking a well thought-out plan, the logistics, and manpower needed for occupation and conquest, Magellan's single-handed decision to conquer the gold islands was outright reckless. The glitter of the gold in the gold islands, an obsession that he had kept in his heart and mind for quite some time, had blinded his mind's eye, leaving limited room for rational thinking. Although his galleons were equipped with powerful cannons, and a lot of guns, arms, and ammunition, the voyage was not intended and prepared for the invasion of new found lands discovered within the Spanish demarcation. Conquering the kingdom of Cebu would turn out to be more complicated than Magellan had anticipated. It would be too late by the time he realized it.

The significance of blood ties, deeply embedded in the age-old socio-cultural and political fabric of indigenous relations, was also another important factor that Magellan failed to consider in the equation. Among the natives, blood ran deeper than the waters of the Pacific. In fact, blood compact was a protocol required in establishing political and diplomatic ties. In many cases ruling families of rajanates and kingdoms were blood relatives forged through marriage. Rajah Si Ayo of Mazzaua, Rajah Kalambu of Butuan-Kalagan, Rajah Umabong of Cebu, and Datu Si Lapu-Lapu of Mactan were all related (Scott, 128, 164).

The three kings therefore were family, and that meant three whole rich kingdoms to them. Mazzaua, Butuan/Kalagan, and Cebu were the gold kingdoms. Goods, especially raw gold, gold wares, and gold products coming from northeastern and northern Mindanao were brought to Cebu, the leading trading center, and from there, traded with other kingdoms in Southeast Asia, China, India, Persia, and Arabia.

Before Magellan's fleet left Mazzaua for Cebu with the King of Mazzaua as the guide, he and his brother, the King of Butuan, had realized the necessity of playing their part in the game of deception that Magellan had initiated. The game of deception would continue in the kingdom of Cebu.

Rajah Si Ayo's Additional Delaying Tactics

During the the first part of the trip from Butuan Bay to Cebu, Rajah Si Ayo led the way in his balangay boat, since he was the guide. However, when they reached Gatighan (Maasin), Rajah Si Ayo slowed down, and was left behind Magellan's ships. *"From the island of Mazzaua to that of Gatighan it is twenty leagues. And leaving Gatighan we went westward. But the king of Mazzaua could not follow us, wherefore we awaited him near three islands, namely Polo, Ticobon (Takloban), and Pozzon"* (Pigafetta, 73). The three aforementioned islands are all in the province of Leyte.

Upon reaching Gatighan, Rajah Si Ayo had slowed down on purpose. Magellan was of course unaware of this. Thinking that the wooden balangay boat was much smaller than their metal ships, Magellan and his men must have thought that the king's balangay boat was really much slower than their ships. Magellan and his men were not aware that the much lighter and ancient wooden balangay boat could sail as swiftly as a bird. Father Francisco Combes (1667,70) said that *"The care and technique with which they build them makes their ships sail like birds, while ours are like lead in comparison"* (Scott, 63). Rajah Si Ayo had deliberately slowed down because he wanted to delay Magellan's arrival in Cebu.

CHAPTER VIII

MAGELLAN AT THE PORT OF SUGBO (CEBU)

"Our ignorance of history causes us to slander our own times."

- Gustav Flaubert, French writer, 1821- 1880

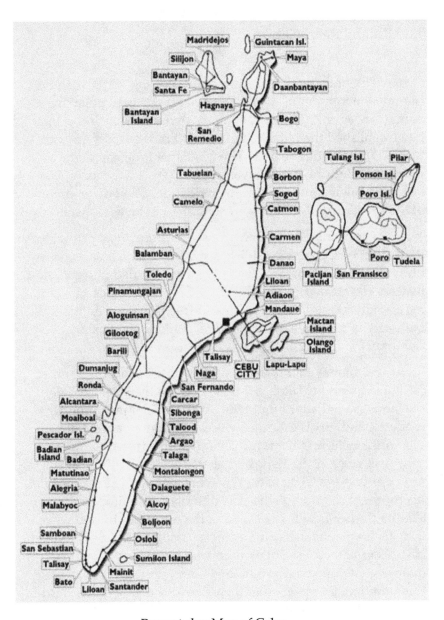

Present-day Map of Cebu

Photo credit : www.jusmaps.org

The Rajahnate of Cebu

The oral tradition of pre-colonial Cebu starts with Sri Lumay, the founder of the Rajahnate of Cebu. Sri Lumay from Sumatra was a Prince of the Chola dynasty from India that had established the Hindu Madjapahit Empire (13th – 16th century AD) in Southeast Asia. The Madjapahit defeated and replaced the Buddhist Sri Vijaya Empire (7th – 13th century AD), based in Palembang Sumatra in Indonesia. The power center of the Madjapahit Empire was established in Java (Hawa).

The Maharajah of Sumatra sent Sri Lumay, a prince, to the island of Cebu to establish a base for the Chola expeditions north of Indonesia. When Sri Lumay settled in Cebu, he instead established the kingdom of Cebu in 1450 as his own independent kingdom, separate and free from the control and authority of the Madjapahit Empire. (Wikipedia, Rajahnate of Cebu, p.1)

Sri Lumay had four sons, namely: Sri Alho, Sri Bantug, Sri Parang, and Sri Ukob. Sri Alho became the ruler of Sialho, the lands named after him to the south of Cebu including Santander Island. Sri Ukob ruled the lands known as Nahalin to the north, including Bantayan Island. Sri Bantug, the youngest son, was ruler of Sinhapola, the middle area of the island, now present-day Cebu City. When Sri Bantug died of disease, his brother Sri Parang, who was described as a limp and who also had other health issues, gave the authority to rule Cebu City to his nephew Rajah Umabong (Humabon). Sri Parang had a son named Sri Tupas who was married to Umabong's daughter (Wikipedia. Rajahnate of Cebu, pp.1, 2). Considering this tradition, it appears that the rulers of Cebu and their families were blood relatives who practiced inter-family marriages.

Sugbo is the original name of Cebu. Even today many native Cebuanos still call Cebu "Sugbo". Pigafetta wrote Sugbo as Zzubu. The "g" in the middle of the place-name Sugbo is a glottal stop which sounds like "ug". Latin-based languages do not have this sound.

The Socio-Political Structure of the Cebu Rajahnate

"In that island are several towns. Their names and those of the principal lords are these: *Cinghapola, Cilaton, Ciguibucan, Cimaningha, Cimaticat, Cicambul. Another Mandaui, and its Lord, Lambuzzan. Another Cotcot, and its Lord, Acibagalen, another Theteu. Another Lulutan, and its Lord, Tapan. Another Cilumay, and again, Lubucun. All these towns and their lords are subject to their king, and each gives him provisions and pays tribute. And after that island of Zzubu is another named Mattan which formed the port where we were. And the name of its town was Mattan, and its lords, Zzula, and Cilapulapu"* (Pigafetta, 84).

The king's men were the chiefs of large **balangay** or **barangay**, the chiefdoms which Pigafetta called towns. A chief was called Datu. The king with the title of Rajah was head of the rajahnate, which was similar to a Greek city-state. The chief's, and the king's, names usually started with "Si" or "Ci" (as Pigafetta spelled it). 'Si' is the indigenized version of the Hindu-Buddhist honorary title "Sri" that precedes a person's name, meaning **"shining bright"** or **"radiant light"**. It is a title prefix placed before people's names to acknowledge the divine light or divinity within each person. Most of the names of the Cebu chieftains that Enrique dictated to Pigafetta begin with "Ci", such as Cilapulapu (Si Lapu-Lapu), Cicambul (Si Kambul), and Cimaticat (Si Maticat). Likewise, Pigafetta wrote the name of the Rajah of Madjawa (Mazzaua) as Siaiu (Si Ayo/Si Ayu). As a matter of fact, when Filipinos today speak of a third person they use "Si" before the person's name.

When Magellan's voyage came to Cebu in 1521, the Rajahnate of Cebu was a kingdom with its central seat of power and governance in the port city of Cebu. There were at least fifteen chiefdoms under the protection of the Rajah of Cebu, based on Pigafetta's preceding account. All these towns or chiefdoms and their chiefs (datu) belonged to the rajahnate, under the king's authority, and paid tribute in currency (usually gold) and provisions to the king. The names of some of the towns, such as Mactan, Cotcot and Mandaui, still exist today.

The location of the Cebu Port in the central part of the Philippine islands, and the port's safe harbor protected by Mactan island to the east, meant it became the largest and best trading center in Mindanao, the Vizzaya islands, southern Luzon and Manila. Gold, agricultural and forest products from the kingdoms of Mazzaua and Butuan-Kalagan were brought to Cebu, and traded with the products of the other Vizzayan islands, southern Mindanao, Maynilad, (Manila), southern Luzon, and the other kingdoms or countries in southeast Asia, China, Japan, India, and Arabia.

Magellan's Aggressive Arrival in Cebu

Upon entering the port of Cebu on Sunday April 7, 1521, Magellan immediately went into an aggressive mode, as clearly described in Pigafetta's own words: *"On Sunday the seventh of April, about noon, we entered the port of Zzubu, having passed by many villages, where we saw some houses which were built on trees. And nearing the principal town the captain-general ordered all the ships to put out their flags. Then we lowered the sails as is done when one is about to fight, and fired all the artillery, at which the people of those places were in great fear"* (Pigafetta, 73).

Magellan ordered his men to raise all the flags on their ships, lower all the sails as if to fight in war, and fired all the artillery from all the cannons on their ships. This display of firepower definitely looked like the Port of Cebu was under attack. Rajah Humabon, the King of Cebu, and his people would have perceived Magellan's arrival as an invasion. Although the artillery from the cannons of Magellan's fleet did not land on the port, Magellan entered the kingdom of Cebu with the sure intent to intimidate the natives with a bombastic, frightening show of force, and firepower. After this,

Magellan sent his foster son, Pigafetta, and Enrique the interpreter ashore.

Meeting Rajah Humabon (Umabong), King of Cebu

On the king's courtyard, they met Rajah Humabon (Umabong), the King of Cebu. "*The captain sent a young man, his foster son, with the interpreter to the king of that island of Zzubu. And when they came to the town they found a great number of men and their king with them, all frightened by the artillery which had been fired*" (Pigafetta, 73). The preceding statement of Pigafetta shows that Rajah Humabon, his chiefs, and the warriors of the different Cebu chiefdoms had gathered in masse at the king's courtyard and were ready and waiting for Magellan's arrival, and possible invasion. Days before, the King of Cebu had already been secretly warned by the advance party sent to Cebu by the Rajah of Mazzaua and the Rajah of Butuan-Kalagan to prepare for a possible attack from Magellan's fleet. Given the explosive entrance of Magellan's ships at the Cebu harbor, it appears the king, all the chiefs of the towns, and their warriors were all upset.

Magellan's foster son, through the interpreter, explained that the firing of the artillery was their custom upon arrival in foreign ports as a token of peace and friendship, and to give honor to the King of Cebu. Delivering a terrifying threat, then claiming that it is a sign of friendship, was a mixed message carrying an extreme contradiction which Magellan probably thought could effectively derail the mental and emotional state of the people and the King of Cebu,

The show of force and superior firepower was also a raw and explicit demonstration of the capacity of Magellan's fleet to demolish the Port and city of Cebu. Entering the port city in a very aggressive manner had the deliberate intention to intimidate the natives and drive terror into their hearts.

Through one of his men, Rajah Humabon asked Magellan's messengers why they had come and what they were looking for. Here it should be noted that Rajah Humabon did not speak directly with Magellan's messengers, but through one of his chief men, who was the king's spokesman. This was royal protocol. The king reserved the right of his rank and authority to speak directly only with those of higher or equal rank. Magellan's foster son, through Enrique the interpreter, said that they were on their way to discover the Moluccas and they were just passing by to get provisions and replenish their merchandise. Rajah Humabon replied and said that they were welcome, but told them that all ships that arrive and dock at the Port of Cebu have to pay customary tribute and port docking fees. The king cited as an example the ship from Ciama (Siam), full of slaves and gold, that just four days earlier had paid tribute to him. Rajah Humabon explained further through his spokesman that a moor (Muslim) merchant who was on the ship from Siam stayed behind to trade with more gold and slaves.

In response to what the king's spokesperson said, Enrique, Magellan's Cebuano-speaking interpreter, said that **Magellan was captain of the greatest king in the world, and therefore** *"would not pay tribute to any other lord in the world."* The interpreter added that if King Humabon wanted peace, he would have peace, and if he wanted war, he would have war. Then the Moro merchant told the king that the foreigners who have come are the conquerors of Calicut in India and Malacca. To treat them well would be to the king's benefit, and if they are treated badly, they will be very bad, as they were in Calicut and Malacca. Adding to what the Moro merchant had said, the interpreter told the King of Cebu, that Captain Magellan's king was even more powerful than the King of Portugal, and that if he did not want to be his friend, the captain *"will send so many of his men against him and would destroy him"* (Pigafetta, 75). Confronted with the serious threat of imminent destruction from a foreign invader with superior firepower, the King of Cebu (Sugbo) replied that he needed to discuss the issues at hand with his council, and would give his answer the following day.

The Role of the Rajah of Mazzaua in the
Cebu Conspiracy

When Magellan's foster son, Enrique, and Pigafetta returned to Magellan's ship, they told Magellan all the things that they discussed with Rajah Humabon, the King of Cebu, and his principal men. After this, Rajah Si Ayo, the King of Mazzaua, who was on Magellan's ship, expressed his desire to go ashore and speak with the King of Cebu. *"And the King of Mazzaua (being in the captain's ship), who was considered as the first king, after the King of Zzubu, and the lord of many islands, went ashore to relate to the said king the honorable character and courtesy of the captain"* (Pigafetta, 75). This account of Pigafetta conveys that Magellan perceived the King of Mazzaua as a diplomat, a man with the credentials of no less than king and lord of many islands, someone who could speak for Magellan and vouch for his character to the King of Cebu. Having shown only hospitality and cooperation towards Magellan and his men during their visit in Baug and Butuan, Rajah Si Ayo, who also guided Magellan's fleet to Cebu, had earned Magellan's approval as a highly credible spokesperson between him and the King of Cebu. Magellan's perception of the King of Mazzaua, however, would later prove to be a terrible mistake. Magellan had no clue that the King of Mazzaua was just playing along with his game of deception. Rajah Si Ayo was in fact the mastermind of the conspiracy.

When Rajah Si Ayo went ashore, he immediately met with his blood relative, Rajah Humabon, the King of Cebu. The meeting was urgent and crucial. It was the first opportunity for them to come together face-to-face and plot the conspiracy. During this meeting, they must have discussed and planned the details of how to deal with Magellan with utmost diplomacy until the time came to strike and get rid of him.

The following day, Monday, the 8th of April, Magellan's messengers went to the town to see the king. "*On Monday morning, our notary, went with the interpreter into the said town of Zzubu, and the king, accompanied by the leading men of his kingdom, came to the square, where he made our men sit down near him, and asked them whether there was more than one captain in all the ships, and whether he desired that the king pay tribute to the Emperor his master. To which our men replied, no, but that the captain wished only to trade in the things which he carried with the people of his country, and not with others. Thereupon the king said that he was content, and that if the captain wished to be his friend, as a greater token of love he would send him a little of his blood, from the right arm, and that the captain should do likewise. And our men answered that they would do it. Moreover he told them that all the captains who came into his country had been accustomed to make him a present, and he to them, and that they should therefore ask their captain if he would observe the custom. And our men said, yes, but that since he wished to maintain the custom, he should begin by making a present, and afterward the captain would do what was due*" (Pigafetta, 75).

At this meeting in the preceding narrative, Rajah Humabon, while trying to assess the fighting capability of Magellan's fleet when he asked whether there were other captains on the two other ships, was noticeably already very agreeable. Rajah Humabon even expressed deference to Magellan's wishes. This time, the king no longer mentioned the customary tribute and port fees that Magellan's fleet was required to pay for docking at the Port of Cebu. Instead, Rajah Humabon asked Magellan's representatives if Magellan wanted him to give tribute to their Spanish Emperor. This was a complete reversal of Rajah Humabon from his position on the first meeting with Magellan's representatives.

Rajah Humabon's accommodating and compromising attitude was obviously the result of his meeting with Rajah Si Ayo the day before. This happened right after Rajah Si Ayo went ashore from Magellan's ship, after Magellan's foster son, Pigafetta, and the interpreter had had their first meeting with the king. During their meeting, Rajah Si Ayo and Rajah Humabon had the time and opportunity to discuss their options, while playing their part in the game of deception that Magellan had initiated. This required agreeing with Magellan's demands and wishes while secretly plotting strategies that would lure Magellan to a battle that he could not win.

Magellan Delivers More Threats

The King of Mazzaua returned to Magellan's ship two days later on Tuesday, April 9, 1521. *"On Tuesday morning following, the king of Mazzaua with the moor came to the ship, and greeted the captain on behalf of the king of Zzubu, and told him that the king was preparing as many provisions as he could to make him a present of them, and that after dinner he would send two of his nephews with other notable men to make peace with him"* (Pigafetta, 76).

Here, the King of Mazzaua was performing the job of a diplomat as he was delivering a message from the King of Cebu to Magellan. The following is Magellan's response to the message of the King of Cebu. *"Then the captain had one of his men armed with his own harness, and made it known that we should all fight this way. At this the Moorish merchant was much astonished. But the captain told him that he was not to be afraid, and that our weapons were mild to our friends, and sharp to our enemies..."* (Pigafetta, 76).

In response to the friendly message of the King of Cebu, Magellan again delivered yet another threat. While the Moro merchant showed alarm and fear, Rajah Si Ayo, the King of Mazzaua, kept a calm composure, just as he had always done since the first day of his meeting with Magellan.

After all, he and his cousin, the King of Cebu, had already had two days to plan a smart defense and offense against Magellan. The plot was to show goodwill and willingness to go along with Magellan's wishes until the right time came to gain the upper hand and strike him with impunity.

Magellan Becomes an Evangelist

After dinner, Rajah Si Ayo, the King of Mazzaua, came again to Magellan's ship with Prince Tupas (the king's cousin), the Moro, the governor, the constable, and eight of the king's chiefs. They told Magellan that the King of Zzubu (Cebu) had given them authority to make peace with Magellan. At this meeting, Magellan started to talk about Christianity, a radical departure from his usual threats of war. On this occasion, Magellan started to convert the natives to the Christian faith.

Magellan saw the need to use the strategy of conversion to Christianity as a means to subjugate the natives. He must have realized that an all-out war against the kingdom would not be smart. Even with superior arms and firepower, his men were outnumbered. His men also knew, that was not the purpose of the voyage, and they were not psychologically prepared for war. Magellan also probably considered that destroying the port and city of Cebu would be severely disruptive and counterproductive. The preservation of the physical integrity of the port was necessary to maintain its trading and economic activities. This would be to his benefit once he was able to take control of the port and the kingdom of Cebu.

Considering his options, Magellan must have thought the smart strategy was to subjugate the natives through a combination of threats against them and their conversion to the Christian faith. So, Magellan decided to use the cross along with serious intimidation. By the necessity of his own motives of conquest, Magellan suddenly became an evangelist. He started by telling the natives the biblical story of

114

Adam and Eve, and some parts of the Christian doctrine. *"Then he showed them several other things touching our faith, which those people heard gladly, and begged the captain to leave them two men, or at least one, to teach them and unfold the Christian faith, and that they would give them good company and great honor. To which the captain replied that at this time he could not leave any of his men, but that, if they wished to be Christians, his priests would baptize them and that another time he would bring priests and preachers to teach them his faith. Then they replied that they wished first to speak with their king, and then would become Christians"* (Pigafetta, 77).

The preceding narrative indicates that the representatives of the King of Cebu wanted to show obedience and goodwill to Magellan, to earn his trust, a strategy that the King of Mazzaua and his brother, the King of Butuan, used during Magellan's stay in Baug. On the other hand, common reason makes it hard to believe that the natives would simply embrace without resistance a foreign religion and a new king they had never seen or heard about from some other world completely unknown to them that this white foreigner Magellan was inducing them to accept. Their seeming willingness to readily agree with Magellan, and open acceptance of the religion that Magellan brought to the natives was too good to be true. The natives' agreeable and accommodating behavior was simply part of the strategy of deception under the guidance of the King of Mazzaua and the King of Cebu.

The natives did such a good job at the game of pretense that they were able to make Magellan and his men believe that they were sincere in their cooperation and agreement with him. Pigafetta wrote about his own perception of the natives' attitude towards Magellan's efforts to bring them to the Christian fold: *"Each of us wept for joy that we had the goodwill of those people. And the captain told them that they should not become Christians for fear of us, or in order to please us, but that if they wished to become Christians, it should be with good heart and for the love of God. For that, if they did not become Christians, we should show them no displeasure. But those who became Christians would be more regarded and better treated than others*" (Pigafetta, 77).

The last two sentences convey contradicting and mixed messages that would have easily given away the underlying deception on Magellan's part. In addition, the last sentence clearly expresses prejudice and discrimination against those who choose not to become Christians. In other words, Magellan's doctrine promised good things only to those who obeyed him, and only those who became Christians would have the better part of the bargain.

Magellan Prescribes Obedience and Chastity

In his effort at evangelization, Magellan, a soldier and explorer, chose to prescribe the principles of obedience and chastity, two of the basic tenets for the Christian catholic priesthood. Although a strong catholic, Magellan was a trained soldier, not a religious man. Magellan probably thought that by using the two requirements for catholic priesthood, he could not go wrong in his effort at subjugating the natives by converting them to the Christian catholic faith. He started the work of conversion by requiring the natives' obedience to himself and to the Emperor of the Holy Roman Empire, who was also King of Spain.

Then, thinking that he had already covered obedience, Magellan touched the issue of chastity. *"And he showed them that they could not have intercourse with their women without great sin, because they were heathen"* (Pigafetta, 77). In this respect, Magellan failed to realize that he had committed a most terrible mistake. He had touched the nerve of the most sensitive, personal, emotionally-driven, and intimate realm of human activity. To declare that it was sinful to have intimate relations with their women because the natives were heathen (not Christians) was certainly the most ridiculous assault against the natives' sense of being human. This, coming from a total stranger who upon his arrival had made it his mission to tell them what to do and what not to do, always threatening them, altering their view of themselves and their indigenous ways and values. Now Magellan is demonizing their marriages, their relationships with their women, and their basic human need for intimacy. All of a sudden this foreign stranger made them think of themselves as sinners, evil-doers, and inferior beings for having a non-Christian spiritual tradition, and their number one sin was sleeping with their wives and conjugal partners.

Magellan had no idea that community-sanctioned premarital cohabitation was an age-old practice among the Austronesian–Malay natives throughout the islands, centuries before the coming of the Europeans. The Ipugao people in the mountain province in northern Luzon, for example, have the "olog": a dwelling built specifically for pre-marital cohabitation of engaged couples. Formal marriages in some cases happened only after the couple had had several children. Divorce was also practiced (Scott, 143).

In spite of Magellan's grave insult, the natives maintained their act of civility, in order to expedite the peace pact. The exchange of gifts between the natives, on behalf of the King of Cebu, and Magellan followed, after which the peace pact was concluded.

The perfect show of the natives' overwhelming goodwill and obedience was of course a charade which faithfully followed the script of the conspiracy. The natives knew that showing outright hostility against Magellan was not a smart strategy. They knew Magellan would most likely launch an artillery assault which would wreak devastating destruction and mayhem upon the heart of the kingdom of Cebu, its, people, and its port.

The King of Cebu and the King of Mazzaua, who had plotted the conspiracy, however, knew that sooner or later they would eventually have to engage Magellan in a war. The kings, however, wanted to take the battle away from the center of the kingdom. They plotted to lure Magellan to a battlefield where he would fight a battle that he could not win.

Rajah Humabon (Umabong):
King of the Rajahnate of Cebu

On the same day, Pigafetta and some of Magellan's men went ashore to speak with the King of Cebu. *"When we had come to town, we found the king of Zzubu at his palace, seated on the ground on a mat of palms, with many people. He was quite naked, except for a linen cloth covering his private parts, and round his head a very loose cloth, embroidered with silk. Round his neck he had a very heavy chain, and in his ears two gold rings hung with precious stones. He was a short man, and fat, and had his face painted with fire in diverse patterns. He ate on the ground from another palm mat, and then he was eating turtle eggs on two porcelain dishes, and he had four jars full of palm wine, which he drank with reed pipes. We made reverence to him as we presented what the captain had sent him, and we told him by the mouth of the interpreter, that it was not in return for the present which he had given to the captain, but for the love which he bore him. (sic) Then the king wished to retain us for supper, but we made our excuses, and on this we took leave of him"* (Pigafetta, 78).

At the time of Magellan's coming, Rajah Humabon was the king of the rich and powerful Rajahnate of Cebu. He was the number one authority of the whole kingdom, and controlled the Port of Cebu, an international port, and the leading trading center of the Vizzaya islands and Mindanao in the 16th century. Rajah Humabon collected tribute and port fees from foreign ships that came from throughout the islands of Southeast Asia, and China, Japan, Cambodia, Champa (Vietnam), Siam (Thailand), India, Persia, and Arabia. They came to trade at the port of Cebu for gold, spices, farm and forest products, and slaves.

Based on the oral tradition of Cebu, Rajah Humabon was the son of Sri Bantug, and the grandson of Sri Lumay, the founder of the Rajahnate of Cebu in 1450. Besides trade, the Rajahnate of Cebu had special relations with the Rajahnates of

Mazzaua and Butuan. Rajah Si Ayo, King of Mazzaua, and Rajah Kalambu, King of Butuan-Kalagan were his blood relatives (Scott, 283, 128, 129).

The kingdoms of Cebu, Mazzaua, and the country of Butuan-Kalagan were bound together by blood and family ties, forged through interfamily marriages among the nobles of the Vizzaya kingdoms and rajahanates. Rajah Humabon only had daughters. His eldest daughter was married to his first cousin, Prince Tupas, who would later succeed him as the Rajah of Cebu. Rajah Humabons' wife was the neice of Datu Si Lapu-Lapu of Mactan (Scott, 83). The blood ties of these Vizzaya rulers would play a significant part in the native conspiracy against Magellan.

Prince Tupas

After their meeting with Rajah Humabon, Prince Tupas took Pigafetta and Enrique to his house where four girls made very beautiful music and sounds with bronze bells, called kulintang and agung (bronze gongs). *"These girls were very beautiful, and almost as white and tall as ours. They were naked except that from the waist to the knees they wore a garment made from the said palm cloth, covering their nature. And some of them were quite naked, having long black hair and a small veil round their head, and they always go unshod"* (Pigafetta, 79).

The next day, Wednesday, the 10th of April, Pigafetta went ashore to ask permission from the King of Cebu to bury one of the European sailors who had died the night before. The dead man was buried in the center of the square with all the appropriate ceremonies of a Christian burial. In the evening, the same was done for another dead man from Magellan's fleet. After this, some of Magellan's men brought to shore a lot of merchandise from the ships. These were placed in a house with assurances of safe protection from the King of Cebu, himself.

119

Magellan's Gold Policy in Cebu

Two days later on Friday, Magellan and his men showed the merchandise to the natives, and traded with them. *"For metal, iron, and other large wares, they gave us gold, and for the other meaner goods rice, pigs, goods, and other provisions. And they gave us ten weights of gold for fourteen part pounds of iron. Each weight is a ducat and a half. The captain did not wish us to take a great quantity of gold, lest the sailors should sell what they had too cheaply for greed of gold, and he should therefore be constrained to do likewise with his merchandise. For he wished to sell it for a better rate"* (Pigafetta, 80).

During this trading activity, Magellan again wanted his men to show to the natives that their gold did not have much material value. Again, Magellan was careful not to show interest in the great abundance of gold and to make it appear to the natives that their merchandise was more valuable than the natives' gold. He maintained a significant degree of indifference to the gold to downplay its value and importance, lest the natives would know that he had actually firmly set his eyes on the gold long before he had set foot on the islands. The natives, however, especially the two kings and the chiefs, were well aware of Magellan's hidden agenda. It was only a matter of strategy and right timing for this issue to get settled.

The People of Cebu and Their Homes

"Those people live in justice, having weights and measures, and loving peace, and they are men of goodwill. They have wooden scales in the fashion of Pardeca for weighing merchandise. Their homes are built of wood and bamboo, raised on piers, and are high so that you must climb up to them by ladders. Their rooms are like ours, and below them

they keep their cattle, such as pigs, goats, and fowls" (Pigafetta, 80).

Certainly, the preceding paragraph in Pigafetta's own words speaks of a civilized society where native people of goodwill lived in peace and justice, with a good measure of prosperity. The natives knew how to conduct proper business in the marketplace. Pigafetta also noted that the natives lived in homes with rooms like theirs in Europe.

The next day, preparations were made for the baptism of Rajah Humabon, the King of Cebu. *"On Saturday following, the captain caused a platform to be built on the square, decked with tapestry and palm branches, because the king had promised our captain to become Christian on Sunday. And he told him that he should have no fear when our artillery fires on that day. For it was the custom to discharge it on festivals without firing stones or other shot"* (Pigafetta, 80). This time Magellan tried to show courtesy to the King of Cebu when he told him about the firing of the artillery on the occasion of the king's baptism the following day.

CHAPTER IX

MAGELLAN SETS FOOT ON SUGBO SOIL

"There is nothing new in the world except the history you do not know." – Harry S. Truman

Drama on Baptism Day

For the first time since Magellan's arrival in Cebu, he set foot on the land of Sugbo (Cebu). It was the day Rajah Humabon was to be baptized. *"On Sunday morning the fourteenth day of April we went ashore being forty men, of whom two armed men marched in front, with the banner of our Emperor. And as we landed, the ships discharged all their artillery. Then for fear that the people of the country had they fled hither and thither"*. (Pigafetta, 80)

Again the firing of the artillery from Magellan's ships caused significant fear and distress among the natives. This of course, by all political considerations, was not at all a very good introduction to the baptism of the King of Cebu. Altough the day before, Magellan through his messengers had told the king about the firing of the artillery, the king perhaps for tactical reasons had neglected to inform his people.

"Then very joyfully we went up to the platform, where the king and the captain were seated on two chairs, one covered with red velvet, and the other with violet. The leading men were on cushions, and the others on mats after the fashion of the country. Then our captain began to speak to the king through the interpreter, to initiate him into the faith of Jesus Christ, saying that he thanked God for having inspired him to become Christian, and that he would vanquish his enemies more than before. And the king replied that he wished to be a Christian, but that some of his chief men would not obey him saying that they were men as he was". (Pigafetta, 81)

Magellan Delivers Death Threats

The following is Pigafetta's account regarding Magellan's death threats against the chiefs who refused baptism: *"Then the captain summoned all the chief men of the king, and told them that if they did not obey the king (as he himself did) he would have them killed, and would give all their goods to the king. And they all replied that they would obey him"*. (Pigafetta, 81)

Under the threat of death and destruction coming from Magellan, the king's chief men agreed to be baptized. Their initial refusal was a reaction to Magellan's demand for them to submit to baptism, which was a surprise, because to everybody's knowledge the baptism was meant only for the King of Cebu. They had to agree very quickly because Rajah Humabon, their king, must have admonished them to trust him, and to submit to Christian baptism for the sake of keeping the peace with Magellan. The compliance of Rajah Humabon and his chief men to the baptisms would later turn out to be a beneficial strategy in the native conspiracy against Magellan.

Setting Up of the Cross and the Burning of Idols

Before the start of the baptisms, Magellan had the cross set up. *"This said, the captain set up a great cross in the center of the square, exhorting the king that, if he wished to be a good Christian (as he had said the day before, he must burn all the idols of his country, and set up a cross in their place and that everyone should worship it daily"*. (Pigafetta, 81).

Magellan's setting up of the cross on the shores of Cebu was again a way to stake the Spanish claim on the kingdom. His order to burn the idols of the country was a command to the natives to abandon their age-old indigenous spiritual beliefs, which was quite a tall order. Carved in wood or stone, the figures represented the "anito", the spirits of nature and their ancestors. Ordering the natives to destroy these figures was to ask them to commit a most terrible act, that of abandoning their gods and family. Rejecting their gods and their ancestors was totally unacceptable to the natives.

After the cross was set up, the baptism of the natives into the catholic faith started. The first to be baptized was Rajah Humabon, the King of Cebu. Pigafetta tells of the baptism of the King of Cebu and the others: *"And he told him that every hour (at least in the morning) they must come to worship the cross on their knees, and that they should confirm with good works what they said and promised. To which the king and all his people answered that they wished to obey the captain's commands, and do all he should tell them. Then the captain told him that he was clad all in white to show them the pure love that he bore them. And they all replied that they knew not how to answer him for his fair words. And so with these good words the captain took the king by hand, and they went up on the platform. And when he came to baptize him, he told him he would name him Dam Charles, as was the name of his Emperor his lord. The Prince, he named Dam Ferrand, after the brother of the said Emperor. To another chief he gave the name Fernand, like himself. And the king of Mazzaua, John. To the Moor, he gave the name Christopher. And to each of the others a name of his choice. So were baptized before mass, fifty men"* (Pigafetta, 81,82). After mass, Magellan invited the King of Cebu and the chief men to have dinner with him, but with an excuse, the king politely refused.

After dinner on their ships, Magellan and some of his men went back ashore and baptized the Queen of Cebu and forty other ladies. Magellan gave the queen a woodcarving of Mary holding the child Jesus, and a cross. The Queen of Cebu was named Joanna, and the Queen of Mazzaua, Ysabeau. The daughter of the queen, and the wife of the Prince, was given the name Katherine.

"That day we baptized eight hundred persons, men, women, and children." He also described the Queen of Cebu as follows: *"The queen was young and beautiful, covered with a white and black cloth. She had very red mouth and nails, and wore on her head a large hat made of palm leaves, and a crown above made of the same leaves after the fashion of the Pope's. And she never goes into any place without one of these crowns"* (Pigafetta, 82).

Since Si Lapu-Lapu's chiefdom was east of Mactan, he was probably a descendant of Sri Ukob, one of the four sons of Sri Lumay, the founder of the Rajahnate of Cebu. King Umabong's beautiful wife was a niece of Si Lapu-Lapu (Scott, 283). Si Lapu-Lapu was Rajah Humabong's family, rather than his enemy. In fact, unbeknownst to Magellan, the King of Cebu had designated Datu Si Lapu-Lapu to play the role of a renegade chief. After the burning of Buaya, Rajah Humabon must have told Magellan that Lapu-Lapu and his followers had fled to the northeast end of the island of Mactan, which would later become the battle ground where, after being lured into an ambush, Magellan was killed.

The other half of the island towards the west was Datu Zzula's chiefdom. Magellan's surprise attack and burning of the village of Buaya was certainly a serious warning to Si Lapu-Lapu, but it also helped set the stage for the Battle of Mactan, the major confrontation between Magellan and Si Lapu-Lapu.

During the two weeks following the mass baptisms of the natives, Magellan went ashore and said mass daily. He also closely spoke with the King of Cebu regarding the Christian catholic faith, *"to instruct him and confirm him in the faith"*, in Pigafetta's words (82).

The Issue of Unburned Indigenous Idols

One day, Magellan observed that the natives had not burned their "idols" as they had promised on the day of their baptism. On this issue it should be noted that the king's chief men and their followers only agreed to be baptized after Magellan had threatened to have them killed. Magellan had also dictated to the natives the so-called promises of loyalty to the Christian faith and the burning of their idols. To Magellan and his men, the carved or sculpted amorphous images were nothing but idols, but to the natives these carved images, called "bulol" or "anito", were representations of nature spirits, and the life-force in all living and non-living things of the indigenous animistic tradition. The "anito" were also representations of the souls of departed ancestors. The natives believed that the connections and relationships of their ancestors with the living continued even after death. The natives communicated with the "anito" through an ancient ritual known as "paganito" (Scott, 85), invoking the "anito" as well as the ancestral souls to help with the healing of the sick, a good harvest, good fishing trips, warding off evil, and victory in war, to name a few. The Spaniards called the natives **pagano,** derived from **paganito**. Translated into English the word **pagano** means **pagan.**

The Miracle of the Sick Man: A Scapegoat

When Magellan asked the king and his people why they did not burn their idols, they had to come up with a good excuse and a credible scapegoat. *"And they answered that they did this not for themselves, but for a sick man that the idols might give him health. And he had not spoken for four days, and he was the prince's brother, and the most valiant and wise man in the whole island. Then the captain said that they should burn their idols, and believe in Jesus Christ, and that if the sick man had himself baptized, he would immediately be cured. And that if this was not true they could cut off his head. The king replied that he would do so, for he believed truly in Jesus Christ. Whereon we made a procession from the square to the sick man's house, as well as we could and there we found him unable to speak or to move. Then we baptized him, and two wives whom he had, and ten maidens. Then the captain had him asked how he was, and he at once spoke, and said that by the grace of our God he was very well. And this was a very manifest miracle in our time"* (Pigafetta, 83).

This so-called miracle of the sick man was another major episode in the great drama of deception that both Magellan and the natives played with each other. Magellan used exaggerated lies, and even claimed the ability to produce a healing miracle with the cutting off of his head as a guarantee, relying only on his underestimation of the natives, fueled by racial and ethnic prejudice, and a sense of superiority over them. He also knew that under the prevailing circumstances the natives would never cut his head off if his miracle failed to work. Magellan's flare for hyperbolic persuasion only succeeded in giving the natives the opportunity to help him create a scenario that would expedite his promised miracle. Of course the natives knew it was not a miracle, for the man was not even sick. He was merely chosen to play the role of the sick man.

The natives made good in adhering to the theme of the conspiracy, which was to go along with Magellan, agree with him, say what he wanted to hear, and do what he wanted to see. Being caught in the act of keeping their indigenous practice of animism and ancestor-worship was proof of their disobedience towards Magellan. To save themselves from trouble and an untimely head-on conflict with Magellan, the natives needed to fabricate a good excuse, transferring the responsibility of their actions to one person, a scapegoat, to play the role of the sick man. The king, however, chose no ordinary man to play the role of "sick man", for the man is the brother of the Prince and the cousin of the king, making the man a significantly credible character. Thus the "miracle of the sick man" came to pass.

Magellan, himself, was probably surprised with his new achievement and status as a **faith healer**, although at this point, his delusions would have already taken a strong hold of him. While Magellan would have believed that his **"miracle"** had effectively convinced the natives of the power of his Christian religion, the natives on the other hand had succeeded in making him take a good dose of his own concoction, for the natives were already able to make him strongly believe in his own lies. To help make Magellan's healing miracle come "true" the "sick man who was healed" showed signs of consistent recovery in the days that followed.

Reckoning with the Renegade

On the 20th day since the arrival of Magellan's fleet in Cebu, Zzula (Sula), the chief of the western part of Mactan Island, sent a message to Magellan through one of his sons. *"On Friday the twenty-sixth of April, Zzula, the lord of the aforesaid island of Mattan, sent one of his sons to present to the captain-general two goats, saying that he would keep all his promises to him, but because of the lord Cilapulapu (who refused to obey the king of Spain) he had not been able to send them to him. And he begged that on the following night he would send but one boat with some of his men to fight."* (Pigafetta, 87).

Zzula's message implies that the time had come for Magellan to finally confront Si Lapu-Lapu, the chief of the other half of Mactan, the **"renegade chief"** who refused to bow to Magellan. The narrative also explicitly states that Zzula (Sula) had previous communication with Magellan over promises to send a boatload of his men on that very day to help Magellan fight against Lapu-Lapu. Instead Zzula sent one of his sons with two goats, making an excuse that he was unable to send his warriors to Magellan because of Si Lapu-Lapu. Here it appears that in his message Zzula was saying that he had not been able to send his men to Magellan because he did not want Lapu-Lapu to see his warriors on their way to join Magellan in broad daylight, so Zzula would send his men to Magellan at night, under the cover of darkness.

Sending two goats instead of a boatload of warriors to fight with Magellan, as Zzula had promised, was outright ridiculous, just as the excuse of keeping Lapu-Lapu from seeing warriors in broad daylight on their way to Magellan was as lame as a sick animal. Pigafetta and Magellan's men started to sense that something was wrong. They tried hard to dissuade

Magellan from going to Mactan and launching an attack against Si Lapu-Lapu. *"The captain-general resolved to go there with three boats. And how ever strongly we besought him not to come, yet he (as a good shepherd) would not abandon his sheep."* (Pigafetta, 87).

Pigafetta tried to make sense of Magellan's irrational decision by comparing him to a good shepherd who tried to bring into the fold sheep that had strayed. The problem with this was that it was not sheep but the supposed stubborn renegade Si Lapu-Lapu and his followers who Magellan had to deal with. He also had to go to war against them to bring them into the fold.

At this point the conspiracy was coming to its climax. Zzula, the other chieftain of Mactan, who was the leader of the other half of the island, was the most likely character to play the role of Si Lapu-Lapu's rival. To make his role convincing, Zzula had promised to send his warriors to Magellan to help him fight against Si Lapu-Lapu. This, of course, was again part of the script of the conspiracy. Zzula's promise of support to Magellan was just another detail of the game of deception. Zzula never had the intention to send his warriors to Magellan, and his warriors never showed up to fight with Magellan against Si Lapu-Lapu in the Battle of Mactan.

CHAPTER X

MAGELLAN IN MACTAN

"To communicate the truths of history is an act of hope for the future." – Daisaku Ikeda

The Battle of Mactan

When Magellan and his men left Cebu to go to Si Lapu -Lapu's territory on the eastern side of Mactan Island, Pigafetta described the events as follows (page 87): "*But at midnight we set forth, sixty men armed with courselets and helmets, together with the Christian king, and we so managed that we arrived at Mattan three hours before daylight. The captain would not fight at this hour, but sent by the Moor to tell the Lord of the place and his people that, if they agreed to obey the king of Spain, and recognize the Christian king as their lord, and give us tribute, they should all be friends. But if they acted otherwise they should learn by experience how our lances pierced. They replied that they had lances of bamboo hardened in the fire, and that we were to attack them when we would. Then we waited for day to come that we might have more men.*" The last sentence of the preceding narrative indicates that Magellan and his men were waiting and hoping for Zzula's boatload of warriors to help them, but Zzula's warriors failed to show up.

The narrative about events leading to the battle continues with the following: "*When day came, we leapt into the water, being forty-nine men, and so we went for a distance of two crossbow flights before we could reach the harbor, and the boats could not come further inshore because of stones and rocks which were in the water. The other eleven men remained to guard the boats.*" (Pigafetta, 87).

The preceding paragraph tells us that as soon as Magellan and his men stepped into the place of battle, they were already in deep trouble. Their ships were unable to get close to the shore because of rocks along the harbor. The artillery from Magellan's ships would fail to reach the shores to inflict damage on the natives' homes and the warriors waiting on the shore.

The Ambush

When they reached the shore, Magellan and his men found out that more than one thousand warriors were waiting for them. *"Having thus reached land we attacked them. Those people had formed three divisions, of more than one thousand and fifty persons. And immediately they perceived us, they came about us with loud voices and cries, two divisions on our flanks, and one around and before us. When the captain saw this he divided us in two, and thus we began to fight."* (Pigafetta, 87).

Fearless Native Warriors

At this encounter Pigafetta describes an army of agile and fearless native warriors in the following account: *"The hackbutmen and crossbowmen fired at long range for nearly an hour, but in vain, (our shafts) merely passing through their shields, made of strips of wood unbound, and their arms. Seeing this, the captain cried out, do not fire, do not fire anymore. But that was of no avail. When those people saw this, and that we fired the hackbuts in vain, they shouted and determined to stand fast. But they shouted louder when the hackbuts were discharged, and then they did not stay still from fear, but jumped hither and thither, covered by their shields. And thus defending themselves they fired at us so many arrows, and lances of bamboo tipped with iron, and pointed stakes hardened by fire, and stones, that we could hardly defend ourselves."* (Pigafetta, 87).

"Seeing this, the captain sent some of his men to burn the houses of those people in order to frighten them. Who, seeing their houses burning, became bolder and more furious, so that two of our men were killed near these houses." (Pigafetta, 88).

"Then they came so furiously against us that they sent a poisoned arrow through the captain's leg. Wherefore he ordered us to withdraw slowly, but the men fled while six or eight of us remained with the captain. And those people shot at no other place but our legs, for the latter were bare. Thus for the great number of lances and stones that they threw and discharged at us we could not resist." (Pigafetta, 88).

Ineffective Artillery

The artillery from the large cannons in Magellan's three ships miserably failed to reach the homes, and the native warriors fighting on the shore. The ships were anchored far away from the shore due to the rocks in the harbor: *"...and the boats could not come further inshore because of the stones and rocks which were in the water"* (Pigafetta, 87). Regarding this particular problem, Pigafetta (88) wrote the following: *"Our large pieces of artillery which were in the ships could not help us, because they were firing at too long range, so that we continued to retreat for more than a crossbow flight from the shore, still fighting, and in water up to our knees"*.

Magellan's Death

Pigafetta (88) tells of the events immediately leading to Magellan's death with the following narrative: *"And they followed us hurling poisoned arrows four or six times; while, recognizing the captain, they turned toward him inasmuch as twice they hurled arrows very close to his head. But as a good captain and a knight he still stood fast with some others, fighting thus for more than an hour. And as he refused to retire further, an Indian threw a bamboo lance in his face, and the captain immediately killed him with his lance, leaving it in his body. Then trying to lay a hand on his sword, he could draw it out but halfway because of a wound from a bamboo*

137

lance that he had in his arm. Which seeing, all those people threw themselves on him, and one of them with a large javelin (which is like a partisan, only thicker) thrust it into his left leg, whereby he fell face downward. On this all at once rushed upon him with lances of iron and bamboo and with these javelins, so they slew our mirror, our light, our comfort, and our true guide. While those people were striking him, he several times turned back to see whether we were all at the ships. Then seeing him dead, as best we could we rescued the wounded men and put them into the boats which were already leaving. The Christian king would have succored us, but before we landed the captain had ordered and charged him not to leave the ships, but to remain and see in what manner we fought. And the king knowing that the captain was dead, caused the remainder of our men, both sound and wounded, to withdraw, and we were constrained to leave there the dead body of the captain-general with our other dead".

Magellan's Survivors Asked for Magellan's Body

After retreating from the battleground, Magellan's men had dinner on the ships. After dinner, Magellan's men sent the King of Cebu to ask Lapu-Lapu and his followers to surrender Magellan's body and those of his men who died in the battle in exchange, *"for as much merchandise as they desired"*. The natives replied that *"they would not give up such a man, as we supposed, and that they would not give him up for the greatest riches in the world, but they intended to keep him as a perpetual memorial"* (Pigafetta, 89).

Magellan's body was probably in terrible shape, if anything was left of it. It was a group of warriors who had ferociously attacked Magellan. He might have been hacked and cut beyond recognition. It was not wise for the natives to send Magellan's unrecognizable, badly mutilated remains back to his survivors.

138

Immediately after Magellan's death, the survivors of the Battle of Mactan and all the other remaining men in Magellan's ships elected two captains: Duarte Barbosa, the father of Magellan's wife, Beatrice Barbosa; and Joao Serrao, a Spaniard.

The Casualties of the Battle of Mactan

"This battle was fought on a Saturday, the twenty-seventh day of April, one thousand five hundred and twenty-one. And the captain wished to make it on a Saturday because that was his day of devotion. With him died eight of our men, and four Indians whom we had made Christians. And of the enemy fifteen were killed by the guns of the ships which had finally come to our help, and many of our men were wounded" (Pigafetta, 89).

Reflection on the Battle of Mactan

A thoughtful reflection and analysis of Magellan's defeat and death in the Battle of Mactan would reveal the details of the conspiracy. On day one of Magellan's arrival in Cebu, Rajah Si Ayo, the King of Mazzaua, and Rajah Humabon, the King of Cebu, plotted a clever conspiracy designed to get rid of Magellan. They knew war was inevitable between them and Magellan. They needed to engage Magellan in battle, but they wanted the battle to happen at a place and time of their choice. They lured Magellan to Mactan, to a strategic battleground, to a battle that he could not win. They chose the northeastern point of the coast of Mactan protected by natural barriers of rocks and reefs. They knew Magellan's galleons with their powerful artillery would not be able to come close enough to the shoreline, which would effectively prevent havoc and destruction to the lives of the native warriors, as well as the people and their homes in the community along the shore.

The King of Cebu himself went with Magellan's fleet to guide them to Si Lapu-Lapu's territory. Magellan wanted to take along Rajah Humabon (Umabong) to show the king how Magellan and his men fought in war. Magellan, on the other hand, was unaware that Rajah Humabon (Umabong), the King of Cebu, was actually leading Magellan's fleet to the designated battleground of the conspiracy where one thousand and fifty native warriors were waiting, ready for the ambush.

Magellan waited for daylight to launch his attack, unwittingly making the battle situation worse for him and his men. The early morning low tide kept their ships much farther away from the shore. Magellan and his men had to take their skiffs over and above the rocks and reefs until they reached the sand in shallow water, from where they could wade to the shore.

At paddling distance from the island of Cebu, the seat of the kingdom, Mactan's close proximity makes it almost an extension of the city of Cebu. As mentioned by Pigafetta, the two chiefs of Mactan were Lapu-Lapu and Zzula. Mactan had thirty villages or balangay. At least half would have belonged to the territory of Si Lapu-Lapu, and the other half to Zzula. Although not much is said about Zzula, he was probably a relative if not a brother of Lapu-Lapu. The plot of the conspiracy required only one disobedient chief, Si Lapu-Lapu. The conspiracy would make it appear that Zzula was Si Lapu-Lapu's enemy, just like all the other chiefs and the King of Cebu, who had agreed to baptism. Since the King of Madjawa (Mazzaua) and the King of Cebu had chosen the northeastern point of Mactan as the ideal battleground, they had to designate Si Lapu-Lapu, its chief, as the renegade.

The time chosen for the battle was more or less three weeks after Magellan had entered Cebu. During the two weeks following the baptism of the natives, Magellan devoted much of his time talking daily to the King of Cebu about Christianity, always making sure the king and his people kept

140

their promise of allegiance to the Christian God as well as to the Emperor of Spain. Meanwhile, it was also during this time that contingencies of warriors from different chiefdoms of the kingdom of Cebu, and the confederation of Vijaya (Vizzaya) warriors in the Vizzaya islands and Northeastern Mindanao, must have discreetly converged on the designated battleground in Mactan. Pigafetta reported that one thousand and fifty native warriors were ready and waiting when Magellan and his men arrived on the shore. This probably was a terrible surprise to Magellan, who thought he was going to war against only one chieftain with just a handful of followers.

Confederation of Vijaya Warriors

Native traditions speak of a confederation of Vijaya (Bisaya) warriors. The large number of native warriors on the battlefield of Mactan offers an argument regarding the existence of a confederacy of warriors from different Vijaya rajahnates and chiefdoms. The Vijaya nations included the Vijaya islands in the central part of the Philippines, and the non-islamic kingdoms of Northern Mindanao, which were part of the Vijaya cultural region.

Kalagan, the old country in northeastern Mindanao, was the socio-economic, political and cultural center of the Vizzaya cultural area. Kalagan was also the regional capital. Over several centuries, when the pre-Philippines was part of the Sri Vijaya Empire (7th – 13th centuries AD), the Butuan Port in Kalagan was the trade and cultural center of the islands. Although the different chiefdoms and kingdoms of the Vizzaya islands were autonomous, and were not under the authority and control of the Butuan-Kalagan country, they had long-established socio-economic and cultural alliances with each other and the country of Butuan-Kalagan. These alliances continued during the reign of the Javanese Madjapahit Empire (1293–1500 AD) that replaced the Sri Vijaya, and was active at the time of Magellan's arrival. The blood ties of the ruling families and people of the Vizzaya cultural region also kept them united. "The rulers of Butuan, Limasawa (Mazzaua), Cebu and Mactan were all related" (Scott, 283). The people of the northern Mindanao and the Vizzaya islands also shared a regional identity, called Bisaya, and spoke Bisaya (Cebuano), the lingua franca of the region.

A folk tradition in Bohol, an island directly a few miles east of Cebu, tells of the story of Hara Waji, the wife of a chieftain who was killed in the Battle of Mactan. After her husband's death, Hari Waji became the leader and warrior of the Barangay of Maribago. She led other women warriors on horseback, and fought against the early Spanish colonizers in Bohol. During Spanish colonial times, Maribago was renamed Cortez, after the Spanish conquistador Hernan Cortez.

Magellan probably expected to fight against only two-hundred or at most three-hundred native warriors in Si Lapu-Lapu's chiefdom in Mactan, not the one thousand and fifty warriors who were waiting on the shore. However, the one thousand and fifty warriors would be more or less the right fighting ratio against the 200 metal-armored men on Magellan's ships, based on what Magellan had told Rajah Si Ayo, the King of Mazzaua, when they were in Butuan Bay. It appears that the two native kings made sure that the ratio was met on the battlefield, just in case.

When Magellan decided to go to battle against Si Lapu-Lapu, he would have thought that he was going to engage only a couple of hundred warriors, a reasonable number of warriors in a chiefdom or datuship. Given that they had superior arms and firepower, Magellan probably thought going to war with Si Lapu-Lapu was some kind of joke. So despite objections from his men, Magellan, with great confidence, went ahead and launched an attack against Si Lapu-Lapu in Mactan.

The Mysterious Renegade Si Lapu-Lapu

Just as the Battle of Mactan proved a fatal anomaly for Magellan and some of his men, Si Lapu-Lapu remained a mysterious, illusive character from the beginning until the end. Si Lapu-Lapu was not even present at the occasion of the baptism of the King of Cebu and many of his chiefs. It should be noted that Magellan threatened to kill all the chiefs present when at first they refused baptism. Shortly after hearing of Magellan's threat, the chiefs agreed to be baptized immediately. This means that Si Lapu-Lapu was not among those who were present at the baptism, because all the other chiefs who Magellan threatened were baptized and given Christian names. Although Pigafetta mentioned the name of Si Lapu-lapu several times, Magellan and Si Lapu-Lapu, it appears, might never have had a face-to-face meeting or encounter. Information regarding the renegade Lapu-Lapu, the chief of Mactan, primarily came from Rajah Humabon. The King of Cebu simply told Magellan about the chief Si Lapu-Lapu who refused to obey Magellan and himself. Magellan.had decided and acted solely on the information the King of Cebu had provided him about Si Lapu-Lapu.

At the battle scene, it was not one, but a group of warriors who attacked Magellan and killed him. Under the circumstances, Si Lapu-Lapu may or may not have been one of them. But again Si Lapu-Lapu was designated to play the role of the one and only defiant renegade chief, which in itself would have been strange if Magellan had given it more careful thought.

Given the political realities of territorial defense and war against an invasion, it is impossible that only one person in the whole kingdom, in this case Lapu-Lapu and a handful of his followers would defy and resist a foreign invader. This narrative would also make all the others, including the King of Cebu, mindless idiots, cowards, and traitors to their native land. This of course was not the case. The plot of the conspiracy was so well-thought out that its perfection could be perceived as its flaw, had Magellan considered it with some critical thinking.

Based on Magellan's estimation, or rather underestimation, of the natives, he had created his own myths about them. Magellan must have thought that the natives, under threats of death and destruction, readily agreeing to be baptized and verbally pledging allegiance to the Emperor of the Spanish Empire, were basically naïve and most probably simple-minded. Believing in his own myths, due to his sense of superiority, and pre-conceived idea of the natives as inferior, Magellan miserably failed to consider that the natives were capable of plotting a clever conspiracy against him. Magellan had no idea that the people he was dealing with came from ancient Southeast Asian Austronesian cultures and civilizations, and as such had an age-old knowledge and sophistication in war and politics. In this scenario, Magellan became his own worst enemy. His European superiority complex, racism, and prejudice against the natives and their indigenous culture became the liabilities that worked against him. As a result, the natives successfully made him believe in his own deception and lies, leading him to his downfall and death.

CHAPTER XI

<u>MAGELLAN SURVIVORS BACK IN CEBU</u>

"Remember that all through history, there have been tyrants and murderers, and for a time, they seem invincible. But in the end, they always fall. Always." – Mahatma Gandhi

Enrique Refuses to Go Ashore

A couple of days following the Battle of Mactan, Enrique, Magellan's Cebuano-speaking interpreter and slave who had sustained injuries during the battle, refused when told to go ashore and speak with the natives. *"Our interpreter, Enrique (because he had been slightly wounded) no longer went ashore to do our necessary business, but was always wrapped in a blanket. Wherefore Duarte Barbosa, commander of the captain's flagship, told him in a loud voice that, although the captain his master was dead, he would not be set free or released, but that, when we reached Spain, he would still be the slave of Madame Beatrix, the wife of the deceased captain-general. And he threatened that if he did not go ashore he would be driven away."* (Pigafetta, 89).

Enrique refused to go ashore because he was scared. The great number of native warriors at the scene of the battle, a ratio of 100 native fighters against one of Magellan's men, revealed to him that the Battle of Mactan was not just a battle between Magellan and Si Lapu-Lapu. It was a war between Magellan and all of Cebu, and beyond. As Magellan's interpreter, Enrique knew that going ashore to the kingdom of Cebu, after the battle, was a big risk. He was not sure how the king and his men would treat him. He probably thought they would kill him. Under Duarte Barbosa's threats of being banished from Magellan's ships, Enrique had no choice but to go ashore.

When Enrique returned to the ship, Pigafetta noted the following change in Enrique's behavior: *"Then the slave returned to the ships and he appeared to behave better than before"* (Pigafetta, 89). Enrique's disposition appeared better after he went ashore. He was probably relieved that the king and his men did not harm him.

The Massacre of Magellan's Survivors

Four days after the Battle of Mactan, in the morning, the King of Cebu sent word to the captains of Magellan's ships inviting them and their men to lunch. The following is Pigafetta's account about what happened on that fateful morning: *"On Wednesday morning the first day of May, the Christian king sent to tell the commanders that he had prepared the jewels and presents which he had promised to send to the king of Spain, and that he begged them to go with others of their men to dine with him that morning, and that he would give them all. Then, twenty-four men went, and our astrologer named San Martin of Seville. I could not go, because I was all swollen from the wound of a poisoned arrow which I had received in the forehead. Joao Carvalho with the constable returned, and told us that they had seen the man who was cured by a miracle, leading the priest into his house, and for this reason they had departed, fearing some evil chance. No sooner had those two spoken their words than we heard great cries and groans."* (Pigafetta, 89).

Escape From Cebu

Upon hearing the cries and groans of the men who went ashore, the men who remained on the ships decided to leave immediately. Pigafetta wrote (90): *"Then we quickly raised the anchors, and firing several pieces of artillery at their houses, we approached nearer to the shore. Firing thus, we perceived Joao Serrao in his shirt, bound and wounded, who cried out that we should not shoot anymore, for we should kill them. And we asked him if all the others with the interpreter were dead. And he said that all were dead save the interpreter. And he begged us earnestly to redeem him with some merchandise. But Joao Carvalho, his friend, and the others would not do so for fear that they would not remain masters if the boat were sent ashore. Then Joao Serrao, weeping, said that as soon as we sailed he would be killed. And he said that he prayed God that at the day of judgement he would demand his soul of his friend, Joao Carvalho. Thereupon we departed quickly. And I know not whether Joao Serrao who remained behind be alive or dead".*

It should be noted that of the twenty five men who went ashore, two were able to go back to Magellan's ship, and twenty-two were killed. Only Enrique, the Cebuano-speaking interpreter, was spared. It is also important to consider what Joao Carvallo, who returned to the ship with the constable, reported right before the massacre. Carvallo said that they thought something wrong was going to happen **when they saw the man who was cured by a miracle take the priest to his house.** Perhaps the priest was taken by force. The man who took the priest was the "sick man" who Magellan had "miraculously cured". This development only confirms that the "miracle healing" performed by Magellan was a hoax, and Magellan's own deception that the natives helped him to believe.

Making Sense of the Massacre

The massacre of Magellan's men, who had come to the king's courtyard to have breakfast upon the invitation of the King of Cebu, by all rational considerations had rendered void, untrue, and absurd, the friendship, obedience, and co-operation of the king, his people, their acceptance of the Christian faith, and their pledge of loyalty to the Emperor of Spain. The massacre defied reason, and escaped the laws of logic.

A native conspiracy offers the only logical explanation. The mass baptisms of the King and Queen of Cebu, the King and Queen of Mazzaua, all the chieftains, and the hundreds of others in the kingdom were simply part of a grand charade, and the plot of the conspiracy. The natives were successful in making the invaders believe that they had the trust and loyalty of the King of Cebu and his people. For three weeks they patiently and cautiously went along with Magellan's wishes, and played the part of the obedient fools until the right time came to strike Magellan and his men with impunity.

More than Magellan's death, the massacre was an end that completely destroyed whatever remained of the supposed friendship, goodwill, love, and peace between Magellan's men and the people of Cebu. The bizarre turn at the end came about, however, because the story that unfolded like a fairy tale and ended in violent horror was after all, a clever native conspiracy. In the game of deception that both sides played, the natives had decisively won. They had successfully accomplished the objectives of the conspiracy. They had killed Magellan and many of his men. With Magellan, their captain-general, dead, those who survived among his men had to flee from the kingdom of Cebu for their dear lives.

The Burning of the Concepcion

When their ships reached the Sea of Bohol the Magellan survivors burned the ship Concepcion. *"Eighteen leagues distant from that island of Zzubu, at the head of the other island which is named Bohol, we burned in the middle of that archipelago the ship Concepcion, because there were too few men, and we supplied the other two ships with the best things that were in her"* (Pigafetta, 94).

In Cebu, Magellan's voyage lost a total of 32 crew members: the two men who died from illness and were buried in the king's square on Wednesday the 10th of April, the eight men who died at the Battle of Mactan, and the twenty-two men who were massacred in the square of Rajah Humabon's palace.

Journey Back to Mindanao

From Cebu, Magellan's men headed back south towards Mindanao. Pigafetta wrote: "Before the captain died, we had news about the islands of the Moluccas". They probably learned that the general location of the Moluccas was somewhere south of Mindanao during their stay in Butuan Bay.

In the the Sea of Bohol, they burned the ship Concepcion, after transferring to the Trinidad and the Victoria all the things they could salvage from that ship. After the battle in Mactan and the massacre of Magellan's men in Cebu, there were not enough men to man the three ships.

Around midday, they sailed along the coast of Panilonghon (Negros Island), another island in the Vijaya region, where according to Pigafetta the people looked like Ethiopians. These were the Aeta and Mamanwa, the proto-Austronesians, the black-skinned aborigines of the pre-Philippine islands.

CHAPTER XII

<u>MAGELLAN SURVIVORS BACK IN MINDANAO</u>

"I shall return." -Gen. Douglas McArthur

Landing at Quippit

From Panilonghon, they sailed further south and came to Chippit (Quippit), in Northern Zamboanga, on the Misamis border where they met the King of Quippit, Rajah Calanoa. *"And about midday, [after] coasting the island of Panilonghon (in which men are black as in Ethiopia), [f.54] we came to a large island. Its king (to make peace with us) drew blood from his left hand and with it made his body, his face, and the end of his tongue bloody as a mark of the greatest friendship. And we did likewise. I went ashore alone with the king to see that island"* (Pigafetta, 94). *"The king is called Raia Calanoa. The port is good"* (Pigafetta, 95).

From the shore, Pigafetta with the king and his men took a boat to the king's house. It was nighttime when they arrived at the king's house two hours later. While supper was being prepared, a large jar of palm wine was served. The king, two of his wives, very beautiful according to Pigafetta, and two of the king's chief men drank up the wine. Pigafetta excused himself from drinking, and observed that these people did the same wine drinking ceremonies as those that he had observed when he was with the King of Mazzaua.

Gold in Quippit

Pigafetta made the following comment about the gold in Rajah Kalanoa's houses: *"When day came, while dinner was in preparation, I walked about that island, where I saw in the king's houses many vessels of gold, and little food"*. Only rice and fish were served in all the meals during Pigafetta's stay at Rajah Kalanoa's house. While food was meager, gold was abundant. *"The greatest commodity in that island is abundance of gold. They showed us certain small valleys, making signs to us that there was as much gold there as they had hairs, but that they had no iron nor tools to mine it,* and moreover that they would not take the trouble to do so." (Pigafetta, 95).

Mazzaua in Mindanao

Pigafetta made a noteworthy reference to Mazzaua and Butuan-Kalagan when he wrote about the geographic location of Quippit. *"That part of the island is one and the same land with Butuan and Calaghan, and lies toward Bohol and borders on Mazzaua"* (Pigafetta, 95).

Magellan and his men first met the King of Mazzaua on the west coast of the northernmost tip of Mindanao. Quippit is south of Mindanao. This means that immediately north of Quippit was territory that belonged to the kingdom of Mazzaua. From these, one can figure that Mazzaua encompassed a large coastal territory that started from the tip of the west coast of northern Mindanao, and included lands on the west coast stretching towards the south, ending immediately north of the kingdom of Quippit in Northern Zamboanga, facing Sindangan Bay. Mazzaua would include the western coastal areas of northern Surigao, northern Agusan, and Misamis.

Pigafetta Promises to Return to Mindanao, the Island of Gold

When Pigafetta wrote about the abundance of gold in Quippit, he identified another place where gold can be found, in addition to the gold mines in Butuan-Kalagan and Mazzaua. The kingdoms of Quippit, Mazzaua, and Butuan-Kalagan were all located on the big island of Mindanao. Pigafetta made a promise to return when he wrote: *"And because we shall return again to that island, I say no more of it"* (Pigafetta, 95). The "island" that Pigafetta is referring to is the big island of Mindanao, for which he had no name.

CHAPTER XIII

MAGELLAN SURVIVORS LEAVE QUIPPIT IN MINDANAO

"And in that history you are trying to connect to something that once was yours – to something purer, something better, something that you lost or something maybe, that you never knew but that you feel you knew." – Sebastian Faulks, Engleby

Wanderings in the Southern Seas

From Quippit the ships Trinidad and Victoria sailed between a west and southwest direction. Still looking for the Moluccas in Indonesia, without their Captain-General Magellan, and Enrique the interpreter, the two ships were lost at sea. They wandered and stopped in several islands and kingdoms. The stops and visits included Brunei, Palawan, southern Zamboanga, the Sultanate of Sulu, and back to Quippit. Then they took a northeast course to the the city of Maingdanao *"which is in the island of Butuan and Kalagan"*, according to Pigafetta. Maingdanao was the kingdom of Maguindanao, in Cotabato.

Abduction and Death in the Southern Seas

Along the coast of Maguindanao, they came upon a ship called **"binidai"**, which Pigafetta described as like a **Prao**, a warship. Desperately seeking the way to the Moluccas, Magellan's survivors took the ship by force, and killed seven of the seventeen men on the ship who, they would later learn, were all chiefs of Maingdanao (Maguindanao). One of the chiefs, who claimed he was the brother of the King of Maguindanao, told them he knew the way to the Moluccas. They took this chief and his son with them. They abandoned their northeast course, and headed southeast.

Later they stopped in the island of Saranghani, a province in Southern Mindanao in the Philippines, where legendary Bisaya boxing warrior and champion, now a Philippine senator, Manny Pacquiao comes from. While in Saranghani, they forcibly took two men to help guide them to the Moluccas. They headed south by southwest, and came upon several islands. During a stormy night, one of the men that they had captured in Saranghani, and the brother of the King of Maingdanao (Maguindanao), and his son escaped by swimming to one of the nearby islands. The son of the chief drowned.

Reaching the Moluccas

With the help of the remaining guide from Saranghani Island, Magellan's survivors reached the island of Tadore, one of the four islands of the Moluccas, on November 8, 1521. Regarding the great occasion of reaching the official destination of Magellan's voyage, Pigafetta wrote: *"On this the pilot who had remained with us said that these four islands were Moluccas. Wherefore we gave thanks to God, and for our great joy we discharged all our artillery. It is no wonder that we should be so joyful, for we had suffered travail and perils for the space of twenty five months less two days in the search for Moluccas"* (Pigafetta, 113).

In Tadore they bought from the king all the cloves that they could accommodate in the remaining ships, the Trinidad and the Victoria. They also learned that Francisco Serrao, Magellan's close friend and relative, had died less than eight months before. Serrao, who served as the captain-general of the King of Ternate, one of the islands in the Moluccas, was reportedly poisoned by the King of Tadore, who was a rival of the King of Ternate.

Voyage Back to Spain

On December 18, 1521, the ship Victoria started to slowly sail out of the Port of Tadore while waiting for the Trinidad, which was supposed to follow right behind. But the Trinidad sprung a leak and started getting water inside the hull. Despite all their efforts, the Magellan survivors and the native divers who helped them were unable to find the leak. As a result, Joao Carvalho and fifty of the men who were supposed to go with the ship Trinidad stayed behind.

The Victoria left for Spain with 47 survivors and 13 Moluccas natives on December 21, 1521. They sailed through the Indian Ocean, and after many months of sailing, and stopping on islands and other countries on the way, they reached the Cape of Good Hope in Africa, where they stopped for seven weeks. After that they went around the cape near the shore. From there they navigated north for two months without stopping, with just a little rice and water for food. Twenty one of their men died as a result.

Completion of the Circumnavigation

On September 6, 1522, the Victoria, with only 19 men left including Antonio Pigafetta, entered San Lucar Bay in Spain, completing the first circumnavigation of the world. The men made it back to Spain after almost three years. Aside from those who were detained in Cape Verde, and those who died of starvation and disease, others had deserted in Timor, or were killed for committing crimes. The nineteen survivors who made it back to Spain were the following:

Name	Ranking
Juan Sebastian Elcano, from Getaria, Spain	Master (Captain)
Francisco Albo, from Tui, Galicia, Spain	Pilot
Miguel de Rodas from Tui, Galicia, Spain	Pilot
Juan de Acurio, from Bermeo	Supernumerary
Martin de Judicibus from Genoa	Chief Steward
Hernando de Bustamante, from Alcantara	Mariner
Nicholas the Greek, from Nafplion	Mariner
Miguel Sanchez, from Rodas in Tui, Galicia	Mariner
Antonio Hernandez Colmenero, from Huelva	Mariner
Francisco Rodrigues, Portugese from Seville	Mariner

Juan Rodriguz, from Huelva	Mariner
Diego Carmena, from Baiona, Galicia	Mariner
Hans of Aachen	Gunner
Juan de Arratia, from Bilbao	Able Seaman
Vasco Gomez Gallego, from Baiona Galicia	Able Seaman
Juan de Santandres, from Cueto Cantabria	Apprentice Seaman
Juan de Zubileta, from Barakaldo	Page
Antonio Pigafetta, from Vicenza, Italy	Chronicler

(Wikipedia, Ferdinand Magellan: Aftermath and Legacy, p.8).

The Ship Victoria

CHAPTER XIV

POST-MAGELLAN SPANISH EXPEDITIONS

"History is a guide to navigation in perilous times."

– David McCullough

We Shall Return

Upon seeing the many gold vessels of Rajah Kalanoa, the King of Quippit, and learning from the natives that the mountains of the island were full of gold, Pigafetta wrote (95): *"That part of the island is one and the same land with Butuan-Calaghan, and lies toward Bohol, and borders on Mazzaua."* Pigafetta also promised, *"...we shall return again to that island"*. The island is Mindanao.

True to Pigafetta's promise, within a few years, Spain sent several expeditions to Kalagan. The subsequent expeditions were the following: the Garcia Jofre Loaisa Expedition (1525), the Sebastian Cabot Expedition (1526), the Alvaro Saavedra Expedition (1527), the Ruy Lopez de Villalobos Expedition (1542), and the Miguel Lopez de Legaspi Expedition (1565).

(Hannibal F. Carado, Spanish Expeditions to the Philipines, SCRIBD).

The First Four Failed Expeditions to Kalagan
Gold Country

The first four post-Magellan Spanish expeditions were sent to conquer the gold country of Kalagan, but miserably failed. These were the expeditions of Garcia Jofre Loaisa, Sebastian Cabot, Alvaro de Saavedra, and Ruy Lopez de Villalobos. The expedition of Sebastian Cabot never made its way across the Pacific Ocean. When Cabot's expedition reached Brazil, he decided to stop and stay there.

The three Spanish expeditions that reached Kalagan: the Loaisa Expedition, the Saavedra Expedition, and the Villalobos Expedition suffered serious losses and casualties at the hands of the northeastern Mindanao Bagani warriors on the Pacific coast of Mindanao. The Kalagan warriors who the Spaniards learned were also Vizzaya (Bisaya) were formidable fighters.

"The first three expeditions that reached Kalagan lost three boats, two ships' anchors, and dozens of lives." (Scott, 162) Faced with hostile animosity and fierce resistance from the Kalagan natives, the Spaniards were unable to land and settle in Kalagan. They had to find sanctuary in Sarangani Islands where the natives were less hostile.

The Garcia Jofre de Loisa Expedition (1525 – 1526)

Four years after Magellan's death, Charles V, King of Spain and Emperor of the Holy Roman Empire, sent the expedition of Garcia Jofre de Loaisa to the pre-Philippines. Seven ships with 450 men left from La Coruna in Spain on July 24, 1525. (Wikipedia, Garcia Jofre de Loaisa).

Captain-General Loaisa was on the galleon Santa Maria de la Victoria. Sebastian El Cano, the other captain was on the ship Sancti Spiritus. El Cano was a Magellan survivor who became captain of the Victoria, the only ship of the fleet of five ships in Magellan's voyage that made it back to Spain in 1522. The other ships of the Loaysa voyage were the San Gabriel, the Santa Maria de el Parral, the San Lesmes, the Aununciada, and the Santiago. (The Biography, https://the biography.us).

When the Loaisa Expedition reached Patagonia (Argentina) on January 1526, bad weather scattered the fleet. The Sancti Spiritus and the Anunciada were destroyed, and the San Gabriel abandoned the expedition.

The four remaining ships entered the Pacific Ocean from the Magellan Strait on May 26, 1526. Poor weather conditions in the ocean scattered the ships until they were unable to see each other. The Santiago, the smallest of the ships headed north along the coast of South America, and reached the western coast of Mexico on July 1526. The Santiago was the first Spanish ship that made a successful voyage to Mexico from South America on the Pacific Ocean.

The ship San Lesmes disappeared, and may have reached the islands of Tuamotus in the South Pacific where a cross and an old Spanish cannon were later found in 1774. The Santa Maria de la Victoria was already on the western part of the South Pacific, but Captain-General Loaisa died from scurvy on July 30, 1526. His body was buried in the ocean. El Cano who also died a few days later in August was buried in the same manner. The Santa Maria de la Victoria would later reach the Moluccas two months later on September 1526. The Santa Maria del Parral whose captain was Iniguez reached Sangir Island north of Sulawesi. (Wikipedia, Garcia Jofre de Loaisa). Sangir is Sarangani Island on the eastern coast of Mindanao in southern Philippines. Sarangani borders Cotabato to the west, Davao Occidental to the east, Davao del sur to the north, and Celebes Sea to the south. (Wikipedia, Sarangani).

The Santa Maria del Parral ran aground in Sangir. Its crew staged a mutiny and killed all the officers, but the men met hostile reception from the natives. Many were captured and taken as slaves. A skiff full of men from the ship fled north towards Kalagan, but met a tragic fate in Bislig. "One boatload was massacred near Bislig in 1526. Sebastian del Puerto who escaped from the boat was later captured in Lianga Bay by Chief Katunaw" (Scott, 162, 283).

The Saavedra Expedition (1527 – 1528)

The Saavedra Expedition sailed to the Pacific on October 31, 1527 from New Spain (Mexico) with three ships; the Espiritu Santo, the Santiago, the La Florida, and one hundred ten men. Alvaro Saavedra Ceron, the captain-general, was the cousin of Hernan Cortez, the conqueror of Mexico, and the organizer of the expedition.

Two months later on December 15, 1527, the expedition encountered a big ocean storm that separated the three ships. The Espiritu Santo and Santiago disappeared in the middle of the ocean, and were never seen again. On December 29, 1527, the

La Florida came close to the Utirik–Toke atolls, and on January 1, 1528, the Rongelap-ailinguinae atolls in the Marshall Islands in the south Pacific. From there the La Florida continued to sail going west.

On Febrary 2, 1528, the La Florida reached the pre-Philippines in Surigao on the northeastern Pacific coast of Mindanao. Surigao was part of the country of Kalagan. After sailing across the Pacific Ocean for 95 days and 1923 leagues from Mexico to the pre-Philippines, Saavedra became the first navigator to make a successful crossing across the Pacific from Mexico in the Americas to Southeast Asia.

During his time in northeastern Mindanao, Saavedra had visited Sarangani Island three times. While in Kalagan country in northeastern Mindanao, the Saavedra Expedition encountered the same hostility from the Kalagan natives that the Loiasa Expedition had suffered. At least one of the three boats and dozens of lives lost in the first three Spanish expeditions (Scott, 2) must have been from the Saavedra Expedition. Unable to land and settle in Kalagan, the Saavedra Expedition left and sailed to the Moluccas. On March 30, 1528, the La Florida arrived in Tidore where the following year on October 1529 Saavedra died. (Wikipedia, The Saavedra Expedition).

The Villalobos Expedition (1542 – 1544)

The expedition of Lopez de Villalobos sailed from Jalisco, Mexico on November 1, 1542 with a fleet of six galleons, and 370 – 400 men. They reached the Marshall Islands on December 26, 1542. Only five ships reached the Carolines on January 23, 1542 in the South Pacific. Before they reached the Carolines, a storm separated the San Cristobal from the rest of the fleet. The ship's pilot was Gines de Mafra, one of the survivors of Magellan's voyage. The San Cristobal found its way to Mazzaua. (Wikipedia, Lopez de Villalobos Expedition). It should be noted that the kingdom of Mazzaua was part of the Butuan-Kalagan country.

CHAPTER XV

THE PRINCIPAL PERSONALITIES

"Those who have no record of what their forebears have accomplished lose the inspiration   which comes from the teaching of biography and history." – Carter G. Woodson

What happened to the principal personalities of Magellan's voyage in the Pre-Philippines? The list of remarkable players would of course include Magellan (Post Mortem), Antonio Pigafetta, Rajah Si Ayo, Rajah Kalambu, Rajah Humabon (Umabong), Prince Tupas, Datu Si Lapu-Lapu, and Enrique, the interpreter.

Ferdinand Magellan (Post-Mortem)

Despite Magellan's defeat and death at the Battle of Mactan, and his failure to reach the Moluccas, the official destination of the voyage, Pigafetta, out of his deep respect for Magellan, wanted him to be remembered and honored as a great explorer who had achieved one of the most extraordinary feats of the European Age of Exploration and Discovery.

Antonio Pigafetta, the chronicler of Magellan's voyage, vigorously promoted the idea of the First Circumnavigation of the World and its relation to Magellan's voyage, in his efforts to honor and immortalize Ferdinand Magellan. Plagued with profound grief and regrets over the death of his captain, whom he held in very high esteem and admiration, Pigafetta did his best to have Magellan and the memory of his voyage installed in the highest pedestals of world history. Pigafetta did this in his presentation of his narrative account of the voyage to the Emperor Charles V of Spain, and to Lord Philippe de Villiers L'Isle Adam, renowned Grandmaster of Rhodes (Pigafetta. 8, 9). The account of Magellan's voyage would eventually spread throughout the Spanish Empire, Europe, and the rest of the world.

In this regard, Pigafetta may have succeeded far beyond his expectations. Since the sixteenth century, Magellan's name has been attached to the world's first circumnavigation. Added to this, many places around the world, modern-day navigation, travel, business names and concepts, as well as natural phenomena are named after Magellan. The most well-known among these include the Magellan Strait in South America, and the Magellanic Clouds, two galaxies closest to earth in the southern celestial hemisphere. Named after Magellan were the Magellan Probe, which mapped the planet Venus from 1990 to 1994, and The Ferdinand Magellan Train rail car, built for the use of U.S. presidents from 1943 to 1958. A ship in the American TV series Andromeda was named the Pax Magellanic. (Wikipedia, Ferdinand Magellan: Aftermath and Legacy, (2012) p.9)

Antonio Pigafetta

The chronicler of Magellan's voyage, and a well-educated humanist, Antonio Pigafetta, an Italian national from an aristocratic family in Vicenza Italy, was one of the 19 men in Magellan's voyage who made it back to Spain in 1522. He was 34 years old at the time of his return to Spain. The day after his arrival in Seville, he presented the manuscripts of his full account of the voyage to Charles V, King of Spain and the Emperor of the Holy Roman Empire. Underscoring both the terrors and the magnificence of the voyage, Antonio came to the church of Santa Maria de la Vitoria, and faced the king's court without shoes (he no longer had any) and with a lighted candle in one hand (Pigafetta. 9).

Shoes were not available in 16th century Southeast Asia. Shoes did not fit the native's view of themselves in relation to the earth, and as such were of no use to them. Although the natives in the Philippines had bodies covered with gold, shoes were not part of their concept of body wear. Going around in bare feet was the Austronesian animistic way of keeping directly and physically rooted to Mother Earth. Shoes of any shape or size were not available in the pre-Philippines in the 16th century.

During his appearance at the Spanish court, Antonio Pigafetta gave his written account of Magellan's voyage to an Italian pedagogue named Peter Martyr. Soon after, Peter Martyr would instruct Maximilian of Transylvania to write a Latin translation for Maximilian's father, the Cardinal Archbishop of Salzburg.

Pigafetta would also present his narrative account of the voyage to the King of Portugal and the Grand Master of the Knights of Rhodes, translated into French from the original manuscript written in Italian (Pigafetta 16, 17).

Pigafetta's eyewitness account of the first world circumnavigation would make not only Magellan famous but also Pigafetta himself. Pigafetta's new celebrity status in Europe as the journalist of the World's First Circumnavigation, however, reportedly made him uncomfortable.

A few years later, Pigafetta joined the order of the Knights of Rhodes, which would later become the Knights of Malta. During this time, Pigafetta worked as the publicist of the Grand Master of the Knights of Rhodes, Philippe de Villiers L'Isle-Adam. Pigafetta took his full-pledged vows as a knight in 1530. In 1536, Pigafetta valiantly died trying to defend Malta from the invading Turks.

Datu Si Lapu-Lapu

Photo Credit:www.picsunday.com/p/Lapu-Lapu-Cebu-Map.html

The Chief of Mactan, Datu Si Lapu-Lapu has sailed into Philippine history as the fearless hero of the first indigenous Filipino resistance against a European invader. Lapu-Lapu's persona as the first Filipino rebel against foreign domination is a source of inspiration for Filipino pride and nationalism. Impressive monuments of the brave and proud Si Lapu-Lapu stand in present-day Mactan Island, and in the Rizal Park in Manila. Lapu-Lapu City in Mactan Island is named after Datu Si Lapu-Lapu. However, Lapu-Lapu's monuments have made their appearance only recently. In Cebu, Magellan's monument had been in place for many decades long before Lapu-Lapu's monuments were built. The appearance of Lapu-Lapu's monuments, although long overdue, is a positive step in the development of Filipino cultural consciousness and ownership of Philippine indigenous heroes and history. The recent arrival and appearance of Lapu-Lapu's monuments in Cebu and Manila are definitely a break from the stranglehold of a colonial mentality in Filipino minds and culture

175

which, starting from colonial times, has placed more value and importance on colonial icons and ideals.

Rajah Humabon (Umabong), King of Cebu

The family name Umabong, not Humabon, has endured, and still exists to this day in Cebu. The name Humabon was Pigafetta's improvised phonetic spelling of Umabong. In Spanish, as in Italian, the letter "H" at the beginning of names and words is silent. Both Spaniards and Italians also "do not hear" the "ng" sound at the end of the Austronesian names and words, because this is non-existent in Latin-based languages. This explains why Pigafetta wrote "Humabon" when he heard "Umabong".

Except for being mentioned as the friendly King of Cebu, Rajah Humabon's real role as a hero in the debacle of Magellan's voyage has not been reported in the pages of history until now. In fact, the Spanish version of Magellan's voyage in the pre-Philipines, often used as a reference by most Filipino historians, offers serious negative implications regarding Rajah Humabon's character. Biased Spanish accounts regarding Humabon's interactions with Magellan, portray Humabon as a naïve, simple-minded native ruler. Removed from the context of the native conspiracy, Pigafetta's account of King Humabon's persona portrays a spineless coward and traitor, an enemy collaborator who without question and resistance simply and gladly relinquished his authority, as well as the autonomy and freedom of his kingdom and people, to a strange foreign visitor named Ferdinand Magellan and his Spanish emperor on the other side of the world.

In present-day Philippines, and even in Cebu, not a single street, place, or object is named after Rajah Humabon or Umabong. No monument stands in memory of this great Cebuano king. The Spaniards, who forty four years after Magellan's death, conquered and ruled most of the Philippines for 333 years, made sure Rajah Humabon (Umabong), the King of Cebu, was never remembered as a native hero, probably an act of revenge against

Humabon for leading a smart war of subterfuge causing Magellan's defeat and death. It would have been stupid for the Spanish conquistadors to acknowledge the fact that Rajah Humabon was the powerful, potent force behind the clever conspiracy and war that defeated Magellan in his attempt to conquer the pre-Philippine gold islands.

If Magellan's death at the Battle of Mactan was the climax of the native conspiracy, the horrific massacre of 22 Magellan survivors four days after Magellan's death outside Rajah Humabon's palace was the shocking and mind-blowing conclusion. The massacre which drove the remaining Magellan survivors to flee with their three ships from the Port of Sugbo (Cebu), was a bloody demonstration of how Rajah Humabon, a Vizzaya king and warrior, had to finally unleash the power of his fury against the foreign invaders.

Despite Magellan's defeat, the Spaniards claimed an implied victory in the pre-Philippines by putting emphasis on the mass Christian baptism of the people of Cebu, led by their king, Rajah Humabon. Filipinos, who are passionate in their love of music, have yet to sing a song for Rajah Humabon, the unsung hero of Cebu, and the leader of the first united and victorious indigenous Filipino war of defense against a foreign invader.

Today in Cebu there is no Cebuano hero named Humabon, but the family name Umabong has endured. Filipinos with the Umabong family name can now step up, and as the descendants of Umabong they can help get the long overdue recognition for the heroic legacy of this great Cebuano king.

Rajah Siaiu (Si Ayo) King of Mazzaua (Madjawa)

Of the three rajahs of the gold kingdoms that Magellan met, the King of Mazzaua (Madjawa), Rajah Si Ayo, had the most numerous face-to-face interactions with Magellan. These personal interchanges between Magellan and Rajah Si Ayo were constant and lasted for about four weeks, from their initial meeting in Malimono in Surigao, in Baug, the hunting grounds along the coast of Butuan Bay, during the trip of Magellan's fleet to Cebu, and then in the kingdom of Cebu.

Besides being the King of Mazzaua (Madjawa), Rajah Si Ayo in his dealings with Magellan performed the functions of a diplomat, conducting himself in the most noble and peaceful manner in the face of Magellan's intimidations, lies, and deception. In fact, Rajah Si Ayo's diplomatic sophistication and skill was so amazingly good, he was able to make Magellan believe in his own lies, successfully beating him at his own game.

It was Rajah Si Ayo who first understood Magellan's plan to conquer the gold islands when Magellan was still in Baug near Butuan. It was also Rajah Si Ayo who saw the need to plan a conspiracy to get rid of Magellan with his brother, Rajah Kalambu, the King of Butuan-Kalagan, and later Rajah Humabon in Cebu.

Whatever happened to Rajah Si Ayo, the "Brain of the Native Conspiracy"? The last time Pigafetta mentions his name in his book is on the day of the baptisms of the natives, on a Sunday, April 14, 1521. Rajah Si Ayo was baptized and given the name John. Later that day, when the women were baptized, his wife, the Queen of Madjawa, was given the name Ysabeau. In the days that followed after the baptisms, Rajah Si Ayo would have stayed in close contact with both Rajah Humabon, the King of Cebu, and Magellan. Rajah Si Ayo would have continued to deliver messages between Magellan and Rajah Umabong, while closely planning with Rajah Humabon and his chieftains the strategies for the execution of the native conspiracy against Magellan.

After Magellan's death, and the massacre of Magellan's survivors, Rajah Si Ayo most likely celebrated with Rajah Humabon, Si Lapu-Lapu and all of the Cebu chieftains the victory of the conspiracy and war against Magellan and his men who came to conquer Cebu. Rajah Si Ayo had successfully accomplished the purpose of his trip to Cebu, which was to help the King of Cebu plan and carry out the conspiracy against Magellan.

On his return to northern Mindanao, Rajah Si Ayo probably reported the success of the conspiracy to his brother, Rajah Kalambu, the King of Butuan-Kalagan. The two brother kings and their people would have drank laksoy or arak, the potent distilled native wine from the nipa palm, and tuba, the sweet tapped natural wine from the efflorescence of the coconut tree, while they celebrated the victory of the native conspiracy.

Despite his critical and heroic role in the first successful native conspiracy and war against Magellan's invasion, Rajah Si Ayo has remained an obscure personality in the narrative regarding Magellan's voyage in the Philippines. Recovering the story of Rajah Si Ayo, and the clever conspiracy that he planned and successfully carried out against Magellan, will hopefully start things in the right direction towards the long overdue proper acknowledgement and recognition of the heroic deeds of this classic native Austronesian diplomat, a smart war strategist of the pre-Philippines, the Brain of the native conspiracy against

Magellan, and the wise monarch of Madjawa.

Rajah Kalambu, the King of Butuan-Kalagan Country

Although Rajah Kalambu did not go to Cebu with his brother, Rajah Si Ayo, he actively participated in the first part of the conspiracy. He plotted with Rajah Si Ayo against Magellan while Magellan and his fleet were still in the island of Baug near Butuan. Rajah Kalambu also must have sent a large contingency of Butuan-Kalagan warriors to join Datu Si Lapu-Lapu's forces in Mactan.

The king of the richest Rajahnate and ancient country in the gold islands, and described by Pigafetta as the handsomest man that they saw in those parts, Rajah Kalambu was no stranger to war. His tattoo-covered body was a testament to his many war victories. Had an open conflict erupted between Magellan and the two brother kings in Butuan, Magellan would have had to deal personally with Rajah Kalambu, the warrior king of Butuan-Kalagan. Rajah Kalambu was a leader who, through his tattoos, led by example his faithfulness to ancestral traditions. Moreover, his tattoos indicate that he was not only a paramount ruler, but also a warrior king who had earned many of his tattoos for exceptional courage and victory in numerous engagements in warfare. It should be noted that Rajah Kalambu was still the King of Butuan-Kalagan, and therefore was in-charge, during the wars against the three post-Magellan expeditions, causing their failure to land in the country of Butuan-Kalagan.

What could have happened to Rajah Kalambu after successfully resisting three post-Magellan expeditions to the gold country of Butuan-Kalagan? Coming from a long line of rulers from the same noble family who had ruled the Butuan-Kalagan country for five-hundred years and possibly even more, he probably lived to a ripe old age, and died a natural death. In 1565, forty four years after Magellan's visit, a Spanish ship from the Legaspi Expedition was sent to check out Butuan on the pretext of seeking trade. The Spaniards reportedly had trade transactions with Rajah Limanpao, the successor of Rajah Kalambu.

Prince Tupas

The Prince who took Pigafetta and Enrique to his home was Prince Tupas, Rajah Humabon's first cousin. During this visit, Prince Tupas showed his guests traditional native hospitality. Pigafetta wrote about four very beautiful girls who played music using metal percussion instruments: *"The Prince, nephew of the king, led us to his house, and showed us four girls who were playing on four very strange and very sweet instruments, and their manner of playing was rather musical. One played on a taborin after our fashion, but it stood on the ground. Another was striking, with a thick stick wrapped at the head with a palm leaf, the bottom of two instruments shaped like a long taborin. Another was striking another larger instrument in the same manner. And the last, with two other similar instruments, one in one hand and the other in the other. And they struck in harmony making a very sweet sound. (These girls were very beautiful, and almost as white as ours. They were naked, except that from the waist to the knees they wore a garment made from the said palm cloth, covering their nature. And some were quite naked, having long black hair and a small veil round their head, and they always go unshod. The Prince made us dance with three of them who were quite naked. And we had refreshment there, and then we returned to the ship. Those taborins are of metal, and they are made in the country of the Sinus Magnus, which is China. There they use them as we do bells, and they are called Aghon"* (Pigafetta, .79). The natives call this instrument *agung*.

Prince Tupas was the successor of Rajah Humabon (Umabong). Forty four years later, in 1565, when the Spanish fleet led by Miguel Lopez de Legaspi entered the Philippines, the Rajah of Cebu was Tupas. There are still people with the family name Tupas in present-day Cebu, in the islands of Panay, Butuan City, and Manila. Although the fall of the Rajahnate of Cebu happened during the time of Tupas, it should be remembered to his credit that Tupas also played his part in the native conspiracy against Magellan.

Enrique, Magellan's Cebuano-Speaking Interpreter

Magellan's interpreter, Enrique, was the only survivor in the massacre of Magellan's men in the courtyard of Rajah Humabon's palace. A Portuguese named Joao Serrao, who was bound, wounded, and bloody, was allowed to run from the king's palace to the port close to where Magellan's ships were anchored. While begging his comrades to stop firing artillery from the ships which would kill him, the bleeding Serrao was able to report on the status of the men who went to the king's palace. "*And we asked him if all the others with the interpreter were dead. And he said that all were dead save the interpreter. And he begged us earnestly to redeem him with some merchandise*" (Pigafetta, 90).

It should be no surprise that the natives spared Enrique. First, the natives knew that Magellan had acquired Enrique and made him his slave and interpreter. Enrique came with Magellan under circumstances beyond his control. Although he was Magellan's interpreter, neither was he Magellan's accomplice nor was he responsible for Magellan's decisions and actions. The second argument lies in the fact that Enrique was a Vijaya (Bisaya) who spoke Cebuano, the language of trade and diplomacy in the Vijaya cultural region of the pre-Philippine gold islands. When Magellan's voyage reached the pre-Philippines, Enrique had come home to the land of his birth, to the place where his mother tongue was spoken.

Where did Enrique go after Magellan's ships fled from Cebu? Since Enrique was a Cebuano-speaking native and warrior, he probably spent the rest of his life in the kingdom of Cebu in the service of the king, Rajah Humabon (Umabong).

CHAPTER XVI

THE PLACES THAT MAGELLAN VISITED

"A people without the knowledge of their past history, origin and culture is like a tree without roots." – Marcus Garvey

What became of the pre-Philippine kingdoms, and places, that Magellan and his men visited? What became of Humunu (Homonhon), the Rajahnate of Mazzaua (Madjawa), the Rajahnate of Butuan-Kalagan, the Rajahnate of Cebu, and the chiefdom of Mactan? What could have happened to the golden palace of Rajah Kalambu, the King of Butuan-Kalagan? These are questions that would probably appear in the minds of readers. The following information about places in Magellan's voyage in the Pre-Philippines should provide some answers to these questions.

Philippine history from the start of Spanish colonization of the Philippines from 1565 to 1898, and the subsequent American colonization of the islands from 1898 to 1946, is filled with forces that have dramatically and forever changed its core, the indigenous Austronesian society and culture of the pre-Philippine gold islands. Modern-day updates of life in these places offer compelling narratives of the influence and impact of both the Spanish and American colonization of the Philippines.

Humunu (Homonhon Island)

Upon first entering the pre-Philippine islands in 1521, Homonhon was the uninhabited island in Eastern Samar on the north Pacific coast where Magellan had set up tents for his sick men who endured starvation, disease, and near-death experiences across the Pacific Ocean. Magellan and his men spent nine days in Homonhon, where they found wild boars, and coconut trees. The natives of the neighboring island of Zzuluan (Suluan) brought fish, boatloads of coconuts, bananas and chickens, which certainly helped Magellan and his men to recover.

Jesuit friars from several post-Magellan expeditions reportedly came to visit Homonhon. During the Spanish colonization of the Philippines, for more than three centuries, Homonhon Island was not associated with news of any historical significance.

In 1898, the United States purchased the Philippines from Spain for 20 million U.S. dollars, transferring ownership and rule of the islands to them. Five decades later, in 1941, Japan attacked Pearl Harbor in Hawaii and Manila Harbor on the same day. These simultaneous attacks signaled the start of the Second World War in the Pacific, with Japan waging a very bloody, brutal war of aggression against the United States and the countries in the Asia-Pacific rim. A colony of the United States at that time, the Philippines was Japan's prime target in the Pacific.

Tiny Homonhon, an isolated island on the northern Pacific fringes of the Philippines, however, would very quietly become part of an unforgettable historic event in World War II, the impact of which would determine the final destiny of Japan's war of aggression in Asia and the Pacific. Following the landing of Gen. Douglas MacArthur in Leyte on October 1944, and the resulting defeat of the Japanese forces in Leyte and Samar, the Americans constructed a naval air base in Guiuan, the larger island to which Homonhon belongs. The Guiuan Air Base was built to serve as the staging ground for U.S. air strikes in Japan and places north of the Philippines still held by the majority of the Japanese forces. It is said that one thousand U.S. warplanes landed in Guiuan in December 1944, the biggest number of U.S. war aircrafts to land in one day on a base in the Pacific. (Wikipedia, Guiuan Airport, (August 2017) pp.1, 2) and Wikipedia, Guiuan Airfield, (July 2018), pp.1, 2)

Mazzaua and Butuan: Two Rajahnates, One Country

Kalagan was the old name of present-day Caraga, although Kalagan included other parts of northern Mindanao which no longer belong to the present-day Caraga Region. Mazzaua and Butuan were two rajahnates and kingdoms of the Butuan-Kalagan country which was ruled by the same family. Rajah Si Ayo, the King of Mazzaua, was the brother of Rajah Kalambu, the King of Butuan-Kalagan. While Rajah Kalambu was the king of the country of Butuan-Kalagan, he was also the Rajah and King of Butuan, the capital of the country where the prime international port was located. Rajah Si Ayo was the King of the Rajahnate of Mazzaua which had its government center and port in northern Surigao. This would explain the fact that the maps of Abraham Ortelius (1570), Gerard Mercator (1595), and Jodocus Hondius (1640) show Mazzaua in northern Surigao.

The ancient Butuan-Kalagan country included Surigao del Norte, Agusan del Norte, Misamis, Surigao del Sur, Agusan del Sur, and Davao del Norte where the Kalagan language is still spoken in many parts. Pigafetta identified Rajah Kalambu, as the King of Butuan-Kalagan.

The Rajahnate of Mazzaua (Madjawa)

From Homonhon, Magellan's fleet sailed south on the Surigao Strait, and stopped in the Rajahnate of Mazzaua, off-shore of Malimono, a town in Northern Surigao. Mazzaua is 25 leagues from Homonhon, and it is in the latitude of nine and two thirds degrees toward the Arctic Pole, and in the longitude of one hundred and sixty-two from the line of demarcation (Pigafetta, 72). This Mazzaua location in relation to its distance from Homonhon, as well as the map coordinates, points to Malimono, a part of the Rajahnate of Mazzaua in Northern Surigao. The territory of Mazzaua, however, extends down south on the western coast of Mindanao. Pigafetta referred to Rajah Si Ayo as "Lord of many islands". The Dinagat Islands north of Surigao del Norte consist of several islands.

How big was the Rajahnate of Madjawa? As a rajahnate, Madjawa encompassed a large territory. The rajahnate of Madjawa could have been neither Masao, one of the little swampy islands formed by mud siltation in the Butuan Delta, nor Limasawa, a hard-scrabble typhoon-swept tiny island one kilometer wide and ten kilometers long with very limited natural resources located in Southern Leyte.

After Magellan's death, his survivors escaped from Cebu, sailed back to Mindanao, and reached Quippit in Zamboanga. Pigafetta realized the extent of the kingdom of Mazzaua when he learned, probably from Rajah Kalanoa, the king of Quippit that Mazzaua borders Quippit, a coastal area southwest of Mindanao, and also that Quippit is on the same land where Butuan-Kalagan is located. The place referred to as "the same land" on which Butuan-Kalagan is also located is the big island known today as Mindanao, formerly Vindanao. Putting these details together, it appears that the territorial domain of the Rajahnate of Madjawa started from Northern Surigao on the Mindanao Sea, and stretched down along Butuan Bay to Agusan del Norte continuing to the coastal area of Cagayan de Oro and Misamis and ending on the northern border of Quippit in Zamboanga facing Sindangan Bay.

A map that Pigafetta drew of Mazzaua as an island resembles the whole of northeastern Mindanao, and lies south of Bohol Island. Nevertheless, the concept that Mazzaua was an island by itself contradicts Pigafetta's own contention that Quippit in Zamboanga, which borders Mazzaua, is in the same land as Butuan-Kalagan. Pigafetta's words explain that Quippit, Mazzaua, and Butuan-Kalagan are all situated on one and the same land, and that land is the island of Mindanao. In Quippit, after seeing the gold receptacles in Rajah Kalanoa's house and learning that the mountains were full of gold, Pigafetta made a promise that they shall return to that land.

To believe that Mazzaua is an island is a futile idea. Pigafetta, however, was not the only chronicler of 16th century European exploration who made an inadvertent mistake. From Mexico, their new colony, Spanish explorers who first came to the western part of America, drew California as an island on the west coast of what is now the United States of America. The fact is that California is not an island, but is part of the vast U.S. mainland on the west, facing the Pacific Ocean.

Mazzaua (Madjawa): Disappearance from the Map

Mazzaua was located in Northern Mindanao. The 1570 map of Abraham Ortelius is the oldest documentation of the existence and location of the Rajahnate of Mazzaua. It is not known when the Rajahnate of Mazzaua ceased to exist, and became excluded from the modern-day maps of Mindanao. Most probably, the Rajahnate of Mazzaua was destroyed and removed from the map after the Spanish colonizers had gained control of the majority of the Philippine islands, including Northern Mindanao.

During the early years of the American colonization of the Philippines, two American scholars, Emma Blair and James Alexander Robertson, wrote The Philippine Islands 1493-1898, a 55-volume compendium of English translations of the works of Spanish historians and writers who wrote accounts about 16th century Philippine society, people and culture. They also wrote an English translation of Pigafetta's account of Magellan's voyage.

Unable to find the place-name Mazzaua in 20th century maps of the Philippines, Robertson and Blair must have arbitrarily decided that Mazzaua in Pigafetta's manuscript was Limasawa, since its location is close to the Mazzaua navigational coordinates of nine and two thirds degrees latitude toward the arctic pole, and one hundred and sixty-two degrees longitude from the line of demarcation. Robertson and Blair also thought that the "masawa" of Limasawa and Mazzaua have the same pronunciation, but it is not the case.

The place-name Mazzaua has since disappeared from modern-day maps, causing considerable confusion and disagreement among Agusan historians regarding its geographic location, and the extent of its territory at the time of the arrival of Magellan's voyage in the pre-Philippines.

Pigafetta's eyewitness account, originally written in Italian, had gone through several translations in French, Latin, and Spanish before its most recent translation in English published in 1969. Such translations had created different spelling permutations of the place-name Mazzaua in maps and books. Among the spellings, or rather mis-spellings, are Malagua, Mazava, Macagua, Macangor, Masana, Mejsana, and Majawa.

Based on his auditory perception of the word, Pigafetta wrote the name of Rajah Si Ayo's kingdom using phonetic spelling based on Italian sound symbols, and came up with Mazzaua. Pigafetta's spelling has generated different pronunciations. Some say it is "masawa", meaning bright sunlight in Butuanon. Mazzaua could also be **Madjawa** derived from the Butuan-Kalagan word "**madjaw**", meaning good or great. **Madjaw hung Madjawa. Great is Madjawa**.

Pigafetta was Italian. His phonetic spelling of the place-name "Madjawa" is Mazzaua, with "zz" in the middle. In Italian, a word with "zz" in the middle, like "pizza", is pronounced in two different ways. One is "pitsa", the other is sounded out with a very hard "z". Pigafetta's spelling of the place-name "Mazzaua" as he heard it was the best he could invent since the "dj" consonant blend is not part of the Italian and Iberian sound-symbol systems, and the letter "j" is sounded out like an "h". Madjawa therefore would be the reasonable choice for the pronunciation of Mazzaua in the light of Pigafetta's spelling improvisation.

Although Mazzaua has disappeared from the map, the name of Rajah Si Ayo has endured. Pigafetta referred to Rajah Si Ayo as "Lord of many islands". The Dinagat Islands north of Surigao del Norte consist of several islands. Loreto, the biggest island in Dinagat, could have been the residence of Rajah Si Ayo. The biggest town in the Dinagat Islands, the town of Loreto, has a large number of people with the family name Ayo today. People with the Ayo last name can also be found in Butuan, Cabadbaran, and Bohol. Could these people be the descendants of Rajah Si Ayo? The name Ayo has descended in their family lines through many generations and centuries in the area of the kingdom formerly known as Mazzaua. Considering this, people with the Ayo family name in the Vizzaya/Bisaya cultural region are most likely descendants of Rajah Si Ayo.

Likewise, the sea port in Surigao City today, the biggest and busiest in northern Surigao still exists, and reasonably must be the same port of the ancient Rajahnate of Mazzaua (Madjawa).

Baug

From the initial meeting between Magellan and Rajah Si Ayo offshore in Malimono, northern Surigao, Magellan's fleet with three ships followed the king's two balangay boats which in the evening landed in Baug, an island located at the mouth of the Agusan River.

On March 31, 1521, Easter Sunday, when Magellan asked Rajah Si Ayo why food was scarce in Baug, the place close to where they had anchored in Butuan Bay, Rajah si Ayo "replied that he did not sojourn in that place except when he was hunting, or to see his brother, *but that he lived in another island where he had all his family*." (Pigafetta, 71). Rajah Si Ayo's explanation clearly says the following:

1. The place where Magellan's fleet landed was a hunting ground, and Rajah Si Ayo did not go there except to hunt or see his brother, the King of Butuan.

2. Rajah Si Ayo would meet his brother, Rajah Kalambu, whenever he went to the hunting ground, implying that the palace residence of the King of Butuan was in close proximity.

3. Rajah Si Ayo's residence was in another island where all his family lived. Loreto in the Dinagat Islands in Northern Surigao might very well be this place.

The Mazzaua (Madjawa)
Rice Farms in Baug (Magallanes)

Today, rice farms that Pigafetta (71) mentions still exist in Baug (now Magallanes) the former Royal Hunting Ground by the Butuan Bay. The tallest mountain nearby which is easily visible from the Butuan Bay is Panaytayon Hill. At the base of Panaytayon Hill are vast hectares of rice farms. Just a few kilometers north of the island are the rice fields of the coastal village of Kalibunan. On the east side of the island just across the Baug River is Taod-oy Hill which also has plenty of rice farms. The western side of Magallanes Island faces Butuan Bay, and the southern side of the island faces the mouth of the Agusan River. Magallanes is seven kilometers from old Banza (Bansa/Bangsa), upstream along the Agusan River, the location of the palace of Rajah Kalambu, the King of Butuan.

The municipality of Magallanes has a population of 21,000 according to the 2015 census. Not far from its shores, stands a 500-year old Bitaog tree. It is believed that Magellan held the First Mass on Philippine soil under the shade of this tree which has been declared "Centenial Tree" because of its age. The town of Magallanes has a safety match and two plywood factories. The 4,900 acre prawn farm industry which used to be the Philippines' top prawn exporter to Japan collapsed in the year 2001 when the white spot disease decimated the prawn farms. The plywood and match factories that dump their industrial waste into the town's river are the prime suspects of the cause of the disease.

Recently however, on the first week of March 2019, the town of Magallanes hit the news headlines when tunnels of natural gas spontaneously burst through the shoreline of the village of Buhang, shooting up 30 feet high like geysers which later ignited into flames making the shoreline look like it is on fire.

Butuan and Its Port

On Saturday, March 29, 1521, from Baug, Pigafetta went with Rajah Kalambu, the King of Butuan-Kalagan, to the king's palace close to the Butuan Port. Based on the time periods associated with the collection of hundreds of ancient jars, gold ornaments and fleet of ancient balangay boats unearthed in Butuan City in the 1970s, the Butuan Port was an international sea port for at least 700 years, from the 9th-16th century A.D. International trade at the Butuan Port had already been in place for several hundred years before direct diplomatic and trade relations between Butuan-Kalagan and China was established in 1011. Before then, the Butuan Port was already part of the Sri Vijaya–Nanhai trading network in Southeast Asia and China (Cembrano, 26).

Located some seven kilometers from Butuan Bay towards the interior of the great Agusan River, the Butuan Port, the biggest in Mindanao, was safe and accessible from all directions to traders from Mindanao Island, the Vizzaya islands, Maynilad (present-day Manila), and the rest of the island of Luzon. The port's relative close proximity to the Southeast Asian trading ports made Butuan a necessary stopping place for traders from China who sailed south to Vietnam, to the Paracel Islands, then to Butuan before proceeding on another sea journey to the big ports in the Malay Archipelago, and to Malacca, once the biggest trading center in all of Southeast Asia. (Cembrano, 25).

Traders from eastern Mindanao on the Pacific coast, such as Surigao del Sur, Davao, and Maguindanao, traveled north to Butuan through river systems that connect to the main water highway, the Agusan River, that flows out to the Butuan Bay on the west side of the Butuan Delta.

Likewise, the Butuan Port was accessible to foreign traders from Vietnam, India, Persia, and Arabia who participated in the Nanhai trade in collaboration with the Sri Vijaya maritime trading network (Cembrano, 24, 26, 36).

The location of the Butuan port on the banks of the Agu-san River, in the interior of Butuan City, protected the port and boats docked at the port from strong typhoons, winds, and sea surges. The port's location was also militarily strategic. Direct sea invasion was hardly possible. Invaders and pirates from the Min-danao Sea who would attempt to invade the city and the port had to face the challenges of strong upstream river currents. Moreover, they also had to deal with the **Bagani, the military force of the Butuan-Kalagan country** (Scott, 274).

Above all else, gold from the gold mines of Butuan-Kalagan, which was traded at the Butuan port, was the bright beacon that drew traders from all over Asia to Butuan. Traders from India, Persia and Arabia also came for the gold at the Bu-tuan Port (Hontiveros, 78).

After taking note of the gold vessels at the golden palace of Rajah Kalambu, the King of Butuan-Kalagan, Pigafetta men-tioned that Butuan-Kalagan had *"mines of gold which are found by digging from the earth large pieces as large as walnuts and eggs"* (Pigafetta, 69).

The Golden Palace of Rajah Kalambu

Pigafetta visited the palace of Rajah Kalambu, the King of Butuan-Kalagan on March 30, 1521. Regarding this visit he wrote: *"And all the vessels he uses are likewise [of gold], as are also some parts of his house, which was well-fitted in the fash-ion of the country"* (Pigafetta, 69). Considering the abundance of gold in the country of Butuan-Kalagan, it would be reasonable to imagine that the walls of the king's palace could have been cov-ered or decorated with thin plates of gold, and the large posts wrapped in gold plates.

Except for Pigafetta's account, nothing more has been written about the golden palace of Rajah Kalambu. When the Spaniards occupied Butuan in 1573, the golden palace of Rajah Kalambu must have been among the first casualties of the occupation, given the Spaniard's greed for gold.

Caraga Region : Former Kalagan Country

The former Butuan-Kalagan country in the pre-Philippines is now the Caraga Region of northeastern Mindanao. Caraga consists of Agusan del Sur, Surigao del Sur, Surigao del Norte and Agusan del Norte. It still has a rich diversity of marine life, forests, rich agricultural lands, farm products, domestic animals, and wildlife in great abundance. Beneath the fertile lands of Caraga lie vast deposits of gold, and other minerals. Caraga has the biggest iron ore deposit in the world, large copper, chromite and coal reserves, and the largest nickel and gold deposits in the Philippines, according to the Mines and Geosciences Bureau (Caraga Watch, Oct. 2009).

The Lumad People of Caraga

The present-day Lumad (indigenous) people of Caraga, especially those who live in the mountains, are descendants of the native people from the lowland coastal regions who fled to the mountains, jungles, and marshes to escape from the brutal Spanish colonization of the Philippines from 1565-1898. The Lumad consist of the Mamanwa and Aeta, (the black Austronesian aborigines), and the Manobo, the Austronesian-Malay people who came to East Mindanao 1,500 years ago (Cembrano, 21).

When the Spanish colonizers started the colonization of the Butuan-Kalagan country in 1573, they established the Spanish Royal Fort in Tandag, Surigao, which they also made as the capital of Caraga, although Surigao and Butuan remained as one district (Hontiveros, 2004, 176). The Spanish Governor-General of the Philippines, whose office was in the colonial capital of Manila, was Guido de Lavezares, the treasurer of the Legaspi Expedition. Lavezares succeeded Legaspi, who died in 1571.

Although his office was in Manila, Lavezares took ownership of Butuan as his **encomienda**. The King of Spain, King Phillip the II, instituted the **encomienda system** that allowed Spanish officials in the colonies to exact tribute from the people of the encomienda. Fifty percent of the tribute went to the Spanish king, and the other fifty percent was divided among the **encomendero** (the owner of the encomienda), the priest, and the Spanish officers and soldiers. In exchange for the tribute, the encomendero was to provide protection to the people, and help them with their conversion into the Christian faith (Hontiveros, 83). In Butuan, Lavezares did the opposite.

In 1574, Fr. Martin de Rada, the priest of the Butuan Encomienda, wrote a letter to King Phillip II about the terrible abuses that Lavezares did to the people of Butuan. Lavezares waged wars against the Butuan villages when the people failed to give the required gold tribute. The evils of the encomienda system took effect not just in Butuan but also in other parts of Caraga. This started the flight of the Lumad, the indigenous Manobo, Mamanwa, and Aeta, from the lowlands to the mountainous jungles and marshes of Caraga. The abuse and oppression of the people of Butuan continued with other encomenderos who succeeded Lavezares (Hontiveros, 83-86).

The Butuan Revolt

The despair and anger of the people of Butuan erupted with the Butuan Revolt, led by Datu Silongan, the chief of Butuan in 1602. The Spanish encomendero, Don Francisco de Poso, the Portuguese secular priest, Alonzo de Campos, the Spanish officers, and the Spanish residents of Butuan were all killed. Silongan and the Butuan natives left their homes and fled to the mountains and marshes in anticipation of a punitive response from the Spanish military forces in Cebu. Fr. Francisco Combes, a Jesuit missionary, wrote an account of the Butuan Revolt in his manuscript, Historia de las Islas de Mindanao, Jolo, y sus adjacentes in 1667 (Hontiveros, 103, 104,105).

Revolt in Linao

In 1648, the Spanish Governor-General in Manila issued an order for native   carpenters, and contruction workers with their families from all over the islands to come to Manila to work in the construction of Spanish fortresses, garrisons, government buildings, streets, bridges and homes in the walled city of Intramuros. Whether they liked it or not, those who were chosen were forced to go, and were uprooted from their extended families, traditional communities, culture, and ancestral domains.

In Butuan, the natives' reaction to the injustice of this forced relocation manifested itself in the Revolt in Linao, a community 40 leagues in the interior of Butuan along the Agusan River. Dabao, a Manobo chieftain, organized an attack against the Fort in Linao, built by Spanish missionaries and the military authorities from Butuan. Some of the priests and soldiers at the fort were killed, and others who were wounded were able to escape. They found their way back to Butuan City after twenty days (Hontiveros, 126).

The military authorities in Butuan City arrested and imprisoned the chiefs in the Butuan villages, after confiscating all their gold possessions. Others were tortured, hanged and decapitated. Those who were not killed were forcibly sent to Manila to join the thousands of slaves from all the different parts of the Philippine islands (Hontiveros, 127).

The continued Spanish abuse of the natives in Butuan and, for that matter, throughout all of Caraga over the decades and centuries of Spanish colonization caused many Lumad (the native people) of the former Butuan-Kalagan country to escape and take refuge in the mountainous jungles. The Lumad, with their age-old knowledge in social organization, agriculture, fishing techniques, and hunting, managed to survive on their own in the remote mountains, jungles, and marshes without contact with the Spanish colonial government centers in the lowland and coastal communities. The Spaniards chose to leave the Lumad people alone in the mountains of Caraga. They had no capacity to penetrate the dense jungles in the mountains. The isolation of the natives worked in their favor, allowing them to live in freedom and peace, while preserving their ancient Kalagan Austronesian-Malay ancestral traditions and culture.

Meanwhile, the natives in the lowlands had to suffer and bear the biggest burdens of the Spanish conquest and colonization. The Spaniards demolished the indigenous socio-cultural, political and economic system of the former Butuan-Kalagan country, as they did to the chiefdoms in the Vizzayas and Luzon. With the loss of their indigenous culture, the colonized people also lost their identity. Through baptism, the natives were given Christian names and in effect new identities as Christians, not Filipinos. The Spanish authorities used the term **Filipino** to identify Spaniards who were born in the Philippines. *"The Spaniards called the natives of the archipelago Indios..."* (Scott, 6). A vague term, **Indios** failed to connect the natives to a cultural identity or even a geographic orientation. In other words, Indios were people with no cultural identity and homeland. Along with the loss of their cultural identity, the natives also lost ownership of their homeland, which became a colony owned by the Spanish empire.

In Caraga, however, the Lumad, the natives who survived in isolation in the remote mountains and jungles, kept their Kalagan indigenous identity and culture through more than three hundred years of Spanish colonization.

When the Philippines became a colony of the United States, from 1898-1946, the Americans called the people of the Philippines "Filipinos" (Scott, 7). The American authorities introduced compulsory mass education that focused on educating the lowland Filipinos about American history, culture, ideals, and the English language. Like the Spaniards before them, the Americans left the Lumad people in the mountains to themselves.

In 1946, the United States of America withdrew its colonial control of the Philippine archipelago. The Philippines became a republic, a sovereign country. The Lumad in the mountains still maintained their independent isolation, but ten years later commercial logging companies from Manila, some parts of the Vizzayas, and companies owned by ruling politicians in Butuan started arriving in the mountains of Agusan, where they set up logging sites with heavy industrial equipment, machinery, and trucks.

Logging in Caraga

From the late fifties to the late sixties, the extensive logging operations in the mountains of Agusan swiftly denuded the virgin forests, leaving only stumps of hardwood trees that had stood there for thousands of years. While logging millionaires were made, the Lumad people lost the forests, the very source of their life and survival.

Meanwhile, Butuan became the Timber City of the South. The logs from the mountains were hauled in big trucks to the Butuan City Port where the logs were loaded into cargo ships and transported to Japan. The hardwood was made into large crates that held machinery and electronics, exported to countries in Asia and the west, like the U.S. and Canada.

The logging companies left when there were no more trees to cut, leaving the mountains bare with hardly anything left for the Lumad and the natural wildlife, that used to thrive from the bounties of the forests. When the rainy season came, tons of loose soil caused by the erosion of the deforested mountains came down with the torrents of rain to the Agusan River, flowing down to Butuan City. Since then, severe floods have come upon the city while the siltation of the Agusan River has continued. In the eighties the level of siltation in the Agusan River in Butuan had gone up so high, preventing the ships from Manila, Cebu, Leyte, and Surigao from entering the Butuan Port. The siltation resulting from the extensive destruction of the forests of Agusan ended the existence of the ancient historic Butuan Port, which as early as the 7th century was already an international entrepot. Today, the shipping and navigation activities in Agusan are conducted at the port of Nasipit, south of Butuan.

Mining in Caraga

In the late fifties to the late eighties, only a few mining companies operated in Caraga. In the late sixties, a gold mine in Del Pilar, a mountain village five kilometers from the town of Cabadbaran, went into full operation. A couple of decades later, the company abandoned the mine, reportedly because the mine had stopped yielding a profitable amount of gold. When the big mining company left, private individuals with their small-scale mining operations took over the mine, which has continued until today.

Expulsion of Lumad People

The passage of the Philippine Mining Act of 1995 opened the door for a number of multinational and transnational mining companies, which set up large-scale mining operations in the mountains of Caraga, right in the very heart of the ancestral domain of the Lumad people. The Mining Act of 1995 gave the foreign mining operators control of the mine sites with 100% ownership of the minerals extracted, while denying the rights and claims of the indigenous Lumad on their ancestral domain. As a result, many Lumad communities have been forced out of their homes and land. (Caraga Watch: Caraga Mining, 2009).

Gold, silver, copper, iron, nickel, cobalt, limestone, aluminum, and silica are mined in Caraga. A total of 44 large-scale multinational and transnational mining companies operate in Surigao del Norte, Surigao del Sur, Agusan del Norte and Agusan del Sur. Fourteen of these companies operate copper and goldmines. (Caraga Watch: Caraga Mining, 2009).

Environmental Plunder

Making a bad situation much worse, the mining activities have caused serious environmental degradation. Landslides, destruction of water sheds, flooding, and siltation of rivers and streams have resulted from the deforestation of second-growth forests, and the destruction of mountains. Fish kills in rivers, lakes, and the seas, as well as reports of birth defects caused by the indiscriminate dumping of industrial and chemical wastes from the mines, have added to the devastation of the land and its people. As a result, many farmers and fishermen in Caraga have lost the age-old traditional sources of their subsistence and livelihood. The big bulk of the income and wealth generated from the mines in Caraga has gone to the pockets of the mining operators, mostly foreigners, and very little to some of the Lumad people who have been recruited to work in the mines.

The Filipinos who have participated in the destruction of the mountains and the exploitation of the natural resources of Caraga are mostly lowland people, whose ancestors took all the burdens and abuse of their Spanish colonizers, who destroyed their indigenous culture and identity. They think of themselves as a different people from the Lumad, who they consider inferior. Their actions show they have very little or no respect for the humanity of the Lumad, and even much less for their indigenous culture. "Filipinos who had grown up under Spanish domination considered themselves a different people from those who had not. The final triumph in this acculturative process can be seen in the fact that those whose ancestors experienced it are unaware that it took place. It is precisely this social amnesia which today stigmatizes as cultural minorities those Filipinos who resisted colonial acculturation" (Scott, 276).

Philippine President, Rodrigo Roa Duterte in 2018 ordered the closure of several open pit mines in Caraga due to serious environmental problems these mines have caused. The President's action is a positive step towards the protection and preservation of the mountains of Caraga and the lives of the Lumad people. Hopefully, the closure of the open pit mines is just the beginning.

The destruction of the last frontier of the once ancient Kalagan country in the pre-Philippines can spell the complete annihilation of the existence of the Lumad people of Caraga, who in the last five centuries have managed on their own initiative to preserve the culture and civilization of the indigenous Austronesian-Malay ancestors of the Filipino people.

Given the situation that has been unfolding in Caraga in the last two decades, it appears that the ultimate completion of the conquest of the people of the pre-Philippine country of Kalagan, which the Spanish colonizers failed to accomplish during the three centuries of Spanish colonization, is being played out and may still happen. At this critical point, only a continued concern and solution with a concience for the welfare of Caraga and its people on the the part of the present government administration can stop and reverse the destruction of Caraga. More than ever, the Filipino people can not afford to lose Caraga. While Caraga holds an immense wealth of natural resources that other countries can only dream of, the native people of Caraga have also kept alive through many centuries and generations the wisdom, humanity, and soul of the ancient Kalagan Austronesian culture, which is the true and authentic source of Filipino identity.

Cebu: The Legaspi Expedition

In 1565, Spain sent eight ships from Mexico to conquer the pre-Philippine gold islands, with Miguel Lopez de Legaspi as captain-general. When Legaspi's fleet left Mexico, Legaspi carried with him orders from King Phillip II of Spain to colonize the pre-Philippine islands.

Like Magellan before him, Legaspi's fleet from Mexico entered the islands from the Pacific through the Surigao Strait in Mindanao. This time the Spaniards changed their strategy. Following Magellan's lead, Legaspi wanted to start with Cebu, to take control of the best port, the economic and trade center of the islands. After the first three failed attempts to conquer the islands starting with the Kalagan gold kingdom in northeastern Mindanao, Legaspi instead headed to Cebu, for they had chosen it as a better starting point of the conquest of the islands.

The Spaniards must have also realized that after the first three failed expeditions, it was not wise to start the conquest directly in the gold lands of Northern Mindanao. It would be easier to start with one relatively small island compared to Mindanao. Moreover, the Spaniards must have planned to act on the opportunity to exact punitive revenge for the defeat and death of Magellan in Mactan, and the horrific massacre of Magellan's survivors in the courtyard of Rajah Humabon's Palace in 1521.

Miguel Lopez de Legaspi's fleet entered the kingdom of Cebu on February 13, 1565. Wary of the Spaniards, Tupas, the Rajah of Cebu, and successor of Rajah Umabong refused to allow Legaspi's fleet to land in Cebu. Legaspi then continued to sail southeast. After entering the Mindanao Sea that separates the Vizayan islands from northern Mindanao, they anchored near Camiguin Island, where they inquired from the natives where they could buy cinnamon and find some people who spoke Malay, the language of trade in insular Southeast Asia. This was just a pretext, since one of the crewmen named Geronimo Pacheco could already speak Malay. The Camiguin natives informed them that they could find cinnamon and traders who spoke

Malay in Butuan. In Legaspi's official report, dated March 14, 1565, he wrote that they headed towards Butuan, but the tides, current and contrary winds took them to Bohol. On the same day Legaspi sent from Bohol the smaller ship San Juan to check out Butuan. (Hontiveros,76).

At first, Datu Si Katuna, the ruler of Bohol, was suspicious if not hostile towards Legaspi for serious reasons. Just three years before, in 1562, Muslim and Portuguese marauders from the Moluccas came and attacked the former seat of the Bohol chiefdom of Datu Dailisan in Panglao-Dawis. Three hundred people were killed, including Datu Dailisan and nine other chiefs. Five hundred men, women and children were taken captives, and later sold to slavery. Dailisan's wife who was also captured was later sold in Maguindanao for 90 taels of gold. The looted property and valuables included "three hundred taels of gold, two hundred gongs, clothing and merchandise". Following the Moluccan invasion many survivors moved from Bohol to Dapitan in Zamboanga. Their leader was Pagbuaya, Dailisan's brother, who subjugated the Subanon people of Zamboanga (Scott, 165).

The Side Trip of the Ship San Juan to Butuan

Guido de Lavezares, the treasurer of the Legaspi expedition, was one of those who went with the ship San Juan to Butuan, where they found out that the place had an abundance of gold. Lavezares noted in his report on May 28, 1565 that "The specimens of gold, cinnamon, and wax were found in a port called Butuan". Andres de Mirandaola, an agent of the Spanish king, wrote in his report to King Phillip II that "Much gold is found in the island of Vindanao, in the districts of Butuan, Curigao, and Parasao. It is said that much gold is mined there and it the loftiest of all these islands" (Hontiveros, 76-78).

The Blood Compact in Bohol

In Bohol, Legaspi, however, was able to successfully convince Si Katuna that they were not Portuguese from the Moluccas, but Spanish, and that they had come in peace. To legitimize the peace pact, in accordance with native custom and protocol, a blood compact between Legaspi and Si Katuna was made.

Legaspi in the first place did not have the intention to wage war against Bohol. Legaspi did not attack Bohol. The Rajahnate of Cebu, the biggest international trading port and trading center in the islands, was his first and main target. Besides, the Spaniards had probably come to realize that Magellan had a good reason to conquer the pre-Philippine islands by starting with Cebu. Although Cebu was not the source of gold, it was the center of local and international trade in the 16th century pre-Philippines. Cebu is also a small island compared to Kalagan, a country which was more or less the northern half of the big island of Mindanao. Cebu is located in the central part of the islands between Mindanao and Luzon. From that central location in Cebu, it would be easier to conquer the Philippines, starting with the islands in the Vizzayas.

The Legaspi Invasion of Cebu

From Bohol on April 27, 1565, Legaspi's fleet of eight ships sailed to Cebu. Despite assurances from the priest, Fray Urdaneta, who told Rajah Tupas, the King of Cebu, that they came as friends, Rajah Tupas refused to believe them and instead told them to stay away. Of course, Rajah Tupas was right. Legaspi would not take no for an answer. He was there to conquer Cebu. Although Rajah Tupas and his Cebuano warriors put up a fierce fight, their bolos (machetes), spears, bows and arrows were no match for the guns and powerful artillery from the cannons on Legaspi's ships, which demolished and burned the city of Cebu to the ground. Tupas and his warriors had to retreat to the hills. Meanwhile, the Spaniards took over the city.

(Gregorio F. Zaide, & Sonia M. Zaide, Philippine History and Government, All Nations Publishing Co., Inc. (2002) p. 59). Like usual conquerors, they killed, plundered, and looted. (Wikipedia, The Rajahnate of Cebu).

Spanish Gold Frenzy and Greed in Cebu

The Legaspi soldiers wasted no time in looking for gold and jewelry in native grave sites. They learned that gold treasures were buried with the deceased owners, an ancient indigenous practice. The gold frenzy and greed of the soldiers who raided the graves went so far out of control that Legaspi had to issue a decree to define a more organized system of dividing the gold loot. Twenty percent had to be set aside for the Spanish emperor, King Phillip II. The other eighty percent had to be declared before the Spanish officials (Hontiveros, 89). It appears that the eighty percent of the gold looted from the natives' graves was divided among the soldiers and the Spanish officials.

Upon the conquest of Cebu, Legaspi immediately started the work of setting up Cebu as the control center from which the Spanish colonization of the islands could start. Two months later, Legaspi offered to pardon Rajah Tupas and his warriors. From the hills, Tupas and his men went back to the city. Legaspi and Tupas signed a treaty which demanded and required native loyalty to the King of Spain. Although peace, cooperation, and reciprocal trade between Cebu and Spain were included in the terms of the treaty, the agreement was an official document declaring the subjugation of Cebu to the authority of the Spanish colonizers (Wikipedia, The Rajahnate of Cebu).

The Cebuanos were baptized and made to promise to pledge loyalty to the King of Spain. Cebu became the first Spanish colonial city in the Philippines and a bastion of the Roman Catholic religion. The Spanish colonial center in Cebu was later moved to Panay in 1568, and then to Manila in 1571 (Hontiveros, 82).

Legaspi's conquest ended the Rajahnate of Cebu, making Tupas its last rajah. The Tupas family name, however, has gone down through many generations and centuries until the present day in Cebu, the Panay Islands, and Butuan.

Today, Cebu is a modern city and is known as the Queen City of the South in the Philippines. The Port of Cebu, just like it was in the 16th century, remains an inter-island and an international port where trade and commerce continuously go on day and night.

Mactan

Present-day Mactan has a population of 430,000, according to the 2013 census, which is a lot of people in relation to the size of the island. Three modern bridges connect Mactan Island to the Cebu mainland. The island is divided into two parts: Lapu -Lapu City and the town of Cordova. Much of the area of the whole island is part of Lapu-Lapu City, named after Lapu-Lapu, the hero of Mactan. Former Philippine President Carlos P. Garcia created Lapu-Lapu City through the Republic Act 3134, on June 17, 1961.

Mactan is a small island with a surging economic wave driven by the tourism industry and the Mactan Export Processing Zone. The Mactan Airport, and the Mactan Airbase provide efficient and reliable support in the quick transport of local people, tourists, and business people, as well as goods and services to and from the island.

The beachfront hotels on the island offer world class amenities and a variety of fun activities such as swimming, snorkeling, boating, jetskiing, and para-sailing. In addition to its history, tourist attractions include the Mactan aquarium and skin-diving in the fish sanctuaries, where one can swim with millions of beautiful, colorful tropical fish.

On the northeast end of the island is a narrow peninsula which the Spanish colonizers named Punta Engano, meaning the Point of Deception, for this particular place in Mactan was the battlefield to where Magellan was lured and killed in a battle the natives made sure he could not win.

CHAPTER XVII

ACCOMPLISHMENTS OF MAGELLAN'S VOYAGE

"Men make history and not the other way around."

– Harry S. Truman

Magellan's voyage has continued to inspire new ideas and accomplish new innovations in science, global commerce, and navigation today, which points back to the accomplishments of the voyage in the 16th century. The following are among the first accomplishments of Magellan's voyage.

The First Circumnavigation of the World

Magellan's voyage, which was launched to find a westward route to the Moluccas in Southeast Asia, was the first voyage from Europe to cross the Atlantic Ocean then the Pacific Ocean. Starting from Seville in Spain, Magellan's voyage crossed the Atlantic to Brazil in South America, down to Argentina, then to the Cape of Eleven Thousand Virgins where they found a strait that goes to the south of the Pacific Ocean. The voyage sailed across the south Pacific, and reached Guam, then the Philippines.

After Magellan's death in Mactan in the kingdom of Cebu, Magellan's survivors found their way to the Moluccas. From there, the Magellan survivors in the ship Victoria sailed through the Indian Ocean to the Cape of Good Hope, onto the southern tip of Africa, and sailed north along the west coast towards Europe, until they reached Seville in Spain. Magellan's voyage, which came from Europe, crossed the Atlantic to the Pacific, and then the Indian Ocean back to Europe, inadvertently accomplishing the first circumnavigation of the world.

Enrique, a Philippine Native:
The First Man to Circumnavigate the World

What sets Enrique apart from all the other men in Magellan's voyage, including Magellan himself, is the remarkable fact that Enrique was the first man to complete the first circumnavigation of the world. Magellan found Enrique in Malacca after the

Portuguese conquest of Malacca in 1511, and acquired Enrique as his slave. Enrique spoke Cebuano-Vizzaya (Bisaya), the major language of the Vizzaya culture region of Mindanao and the Vizzaya islands in the pre-Philippines. When Magellan's voyage reached the pre-Philippines, Enrique assumed the job of interpreter. Enrique's proficiency in the Cebuano language makes him a native of the pre-Philippines, rather than Malacca. Through Enrique's help as an interpreter, all the vocabulary words that Pigafetta recorded, which appear on pages 90, 91, and 94, are Cebuano-Vizzaya words.

During the time when the Port of Malacca was the biggest trading center in Southeast Asia, many Austronesians, the natives from the pre-Philippines were in Malacca and worked as shipping tycoons, merchants, civil servants, and mercenary warriors. Many of those warriors manned and navigated the ships that protected the Strait of Malacca (Scott, 194).

Magellan acquired Enrique in Malacca, because he needed someone who spoke the language of the pre-Philippine gold islands, the secret destination of his later voyage on a westward route to Southeast Asia. From Malacca, sometime in 1512, Magellan took Enrique through the Indian Ocean to Portugal, then to Morocco, back to Portugal, then to Spain. In 1519, Magellan took Enrique on his voyage from Spain, across the Atlantic Ocean to South America, then across the Pacific back to the pre-Philippines.

Coming back to his homeland might have been the realization of Enrique's dream, but this event took on a much broader significance which Enrique himself may never even have realized. Enrique had achieved a world record. Enrique's homecoming to the Philippines inadvertently made him the first man to circumnavigate the world. Before Magellan and any of the sailors in his voyage, Enrique was the first man to come back to the place where his mother tongue was spoken, after circling the globe.

Enrique was a Mulatto, according to the description in Magellan's Last Will, which makes Enrique an Austronesian-Malay, a mixture of the Negroid proto-Austronesians and the and the Malay-Austronesians, with Mongolian and Chinese genetic admixtures. The Negroid features, dark skin, and tight curly hair of the Mamanwa or Aeta, the black aborigines, were probably pronounced in Enrique's facial and physical features. The Mamanwa, who are said to have come to the pre-Philippine islands, are most likely part of the group of the first modern humans who came from East Afica to Southeast Asia between 60,000-75,000 years ago (D. Cyranoski, Weekly Journal of Science, Dec. 2009).

As the first man to circumnavigate the globe on the great oceans of the world, Enrique, although inadvertently, was true to the age-old tradition of sea-faring and exploration of the Austronesians, the ancient navigators and explorers who colonized and populated the Malay Archipelago, most of the islands in the Pacific, Madagascar, and the Easter islands.

Discovery of the Magellan Strait

When Magellan's voyage found the Strait near the southern end of Pathagonia, the old name of Argentina, they found the passage that connects the Atlantic Ocean to the Pacific Ocean. The discovery of the strait opened the westward ocean route to Southeast Asia. Since it was a Spanish expedition that had discovered the westward route, Spain would have the authority and control over that route, just as the Portuguese controlled the eastern route through the Indian Ocean. Upon the discovery of the strait, Magellan said that he knew about the existence of the strait. He had seen it in the marine chart made by a sailor named Martin de Bohemia for the king of Portugal (Pigafetta, 51). The strait later would be named the Magellan Strait.

Addition of the Pacific Ocean to the World Map

Magellan added to the world map the Pacific Ocean, which is one-third of the world's surface with an area bigger than all the land surfaces of the earth. (Pigafetta, 1).

Magellan Found the Pre-Philippine Gold Country

In Philippine history books it is said that Magellan discovered the Philippines. While it is true that Magellan set foot in the Philippines, to say that he discovered the Philippines is far from the truth. Today that is what is called **fake news**. When Magellan reached the Philippines, he found an ancient Austronesian people, their civilization, and a country of gold. Upon the arrival of Magellan's voyage in Samar, on the northern Pacific coast of the archipelago, they met and saw the natives of Suluan and the Kapri people of a nearby island bedecked in gold, wearing heavy gold necklaces, large gold earrings, gold arm bands, and gold leg bands. The natives had knives and daggers with gold handles and gold-decorated lances. Pigafetta wrote that they called **Homonhon Aguade**, for it was there where they found fresh water, and the **first signs of gold**. They did not find gold in Homonhon Island, but the first signs of gold were the gold ornaments that the natives wore on their bodies. "From the day Magellan first saw gold earrings, armbands, and spear decorations in Homonhon, Spaniards kept reporting gold jewelry in truly astonishing quantities. They were struck not only by its amount and wide distribution, but by the fact that it appeared to be part of the normal attire of persons otherwise naked" (Scott, 32).

After forcing out information from the Suluan natives regarding the source of the gold, Magellan sailed from Homonhon, through the Surigao Strait, going south to the the Kalagan gold country in northern Mindanao, where he visited parts of the kingdom of Mazzaua, in Malimono in northern Surigao, and in Baug near Butuan. Pigafetta, who went with the King of Butuan to the king's palace in Butuan City, saw the king's vessels (bowls) all made of gold, and parts of the king's house which were also made of gold. It was there in Butuan Bay that Magellan learned that the kingdom of Mazzaua and the country of Butuan-Kalagan had very rich gold mines that yielded gold nuggets "as big as eggs and walnuts". The day after Pigafetta visited the palace of the King of Butuan, Magellan, fifty of his men, and the priest said the first mass on Philippine soil on the shores of Baug. The mass was a momentous event. It was the celebration of Magellan's success. Magellan had arrived at his secret destination, the land of gold.

Magellan's Voyage Ushered the Spanish Conquest of the East Indies

After Magellan's voyage, Spain sent five expeditions to the Philippines. The first four expeditions failed to conquer the Philippines, but in 1565, the fifth expedition led by Miguel Lopez de Legaspi succeeded, forty-four years after Magellan's expedition. After colonizing the Philippines, Spain also colonized Guam, the Marianas, Carolines, the Palau islands in the Pacific Ocean, and Sulawesi (Celebes) and the Moluccas in Indonesia (Wikipedia, Spanish East Indies.)

CHAPTER XVIII

<u>SUMMARY and CONCLUSION</u>

"The repeated lies become history, but they don't necessarily become the truth." – Colum McCann, Let the Great World Spin

The Untold Native Conspiracy

Why was the native conspiracy untold? The strange debacle of Magellan's voyage in the pre-Philippines points to two important events never before included in previously written history book accounts of this important chapter in world history. This gross omission is no accident. It can be reasonably argued and attributed to the fact that the writers who wrote the first interpretations of Pigaffeta's narrative account were Spanish friars and historians, who wrote history from their standpoint as colonizers. It is important to note that the once-powerful friars ruled the church-controlled local and national governments of the Philippines during the Spanish colonial regime from 1565-1898. The subsequent American colonization of the Philippines from 1898-1946 failed to make the situation any better.

The Americans installed compulsory mass education based on the curriculum of the U.S. educational system. U.S. history and government was taught in the schools, but no subject on Philippine history. When the United States withdrew its colonial control of the Philippines, on July 4, 1946, the Philippines became an independent sovereign country. Several years later, Philippine history was introduced into the curriculum. The first writers of books on Philippine history, however, appear to have used as a reference the same Spanish version of the arrival of Magellan's voyage in the Philippines, probably due to the lack or absence of other alternative sources. As a result, the Spanish version became the mainstream version.

One of the two very important events omitted in the mainstream version was Magellan's visit to three places in the Butuan-Kalagan country. The first two are in the territory of Mazzaua, namely: offshore in Malimono in northern Surigao, and in the island of Baug by the Butuan Bay. The third is the palace of the King of Butuan in the port city of Butuan, which Pigafetta visited on behalf of Magellan

The second very important event that was excluded from the mainstream narrative was the massacre of 22 of Magellan's survivors in the yard outside Rajah Humabon's palace. The twenty two men who died went to the king's palace upon Rajah Humabon's invitation to lunch.

The aforementioned omissions make it difficult, if not next to impossible, to see the native conspiracy against Magellan. Pigafetta's narrative, a faithful day-to-day eyewitness account of Magellan's voyage in the pre-Philippines, tells a more complete story after I had put the missing pieces of the puzzle, and connected the dots.

An educated man from a noble family in Vicenza, Italy, Pigafetta tried his best to write the daily chronicles from the independent point of view of a journalist. The inclusion of the northern Mindanao episode of Magellan's voyage in the pre-Philippines written in Pigafetta's report is crucial to the revelation of the untold native conspiracy against Ferdinand Magellan.

Success of the Native Conspiracy

The conspiracy of the native kings, a reaction to Magellan's move to conquer the Pre-Philippine gold islands, was a possibility that Magellan probably never imagined. Rajah Si Ayo, King of Madjawa (Mazzaua), was the first native rajah who received serious threats from Magellan. Rajah Si Ayo chose not to show an adverse reaction to Magellan's threats. Instead, he continued to show a positive posture towards Magellan. Magellan probably thought that Rajah Si Ayo's attitude was an inability to comprehend threats, a response born out of fear, or even a submissive, naïve one. Magellan had no idea that Rajah Si Ayo's pleasant attitude was actually the clever use of acquiescent diplomacy with the hidden motive of deception. Rajah Si Ayo would share this strategy with his brother, Rajah Kalambu, the King of Butuan-Kalagan, as they started planning a conspiracy against Magellan, while delaying his trip to Cebu to make time to warn their relative, Rajah Humabon (Umabong), the King of Cebu, about Magellan's possible invasion of the Port of Cebu.

Instead of sending two of his men as guides, an arrangement to which he initially agreed, Rajah Si Ayo himself offered to guide Magellan's fleet to Cebu. Magellan probably thought Rajah Si Ayo's offer was a continued exercise of the rajah's goodwill. In fact, later, when they reached Cebu, Magellan would send Rajah Si Ayo as a diplomat to help communicate Magellan's wishes to the king of Cebu. However, Magellan was not aware that Rajah Si Ayo offered to guide Magellan to Cebu because he needed to discuss the details of the conspiracy with his blood relative, Rajah Humabon. The rulers of Butuan, Mazzaua, Cebu and Mactan were all blood relatives. They married within their families to preserve the continuity of their noble bloodlines in the Vizzaya seats of power. The Vizzaya epic **Humadapnon** explains this marriage protocol among the Vizzaya nobles (Scott, 128).

The day after Rajah Si Ayo spoke with Rajah Humabon, the King of Cebu no longer talked to Pigafetta and Magellan's other representatives about the customary tribute that visiting foreign ships docked at the Port of Cebu were required to pay. Once again, Rajah Si Ayo must have advised Rajah Humabon, and shared with him the strategy of acquiescent diplomacy as the two of them discussed the plan of the conspiracy against Magellan.

Going along with Magellan's wishes was the underlying requirement of the plot to delay an open face-to-face armed conflict with Magellan, while allowing time for contingents of warriors from all over the kingdom of Cebu, and others from the Vizzaya cultural regions, to secretly converge in Mactan, the designated strategic battleground of the conspiracy.

In the meantime, the two kings, their wives, the chief men of the King of Cebu, and even the Cebuano-speaking Muslim trader who came with the ship from Ciama (Siam, present-day Thailand) agreed to be baptized. A few days later, the King of Cebu would inform Magellan that Si Lapu-Lapu, the chief of Mactan, refused to obey the king and Magellan. Rajah Si Ayo knew that Magellan would jump at the opportunity to go to war with the enemies of the King of Cebu. In retrospect, back in

Butuan, Magellan offered to attack Rajah Si Ayo's enemies. Perceiving Magellan's strategy of "Divide and Conquer", Rajah Si Ayo refused Magellan's offer with diplomatic sophistication, telling Magellan it was not the season to go to war against the king's enemies. In Cebu, the native kings, Rajah Si Ayo and Rajah Humabon, used Magellan's "Divide and Conquer" strategy against him, to lure him into a battle the two native kings made sure he could not win.

Magellan's Failure

The first reason behind Magellan's defeat and death in the Pre-Philippine gold islands was the fact that he had a personal purpose, a secret all of his own, and separate from the official purpose of the voyage. Upon reaching northeastern Mindanao, and after confirming that his voyage had indeed reached the gold kingdoms of Butuan-Kalagan and Mazzaua, Magellan made a paradigm shift. He abandoned the official purpose of the voyage, which was to go to the Moluccas, and instead started pursuing his hidden agenda, the conquest of the Pre-Philippine gold islands.

Magellan's paradigm shift, nevertheless, was doomed from the very start. His independent, aggressive, adventurous streak would come into play, but would eventually work against him. Although he was ill-prepared for the daunting task of conquering the gold islands, he wanted to grab the opportunity without delay, ignoring a realistic assessment of the pros and cons of the situation. He chose to abandon the official purpose of the voyage, and start the conquest of the pre-Philippine gold islands.

To say that Magellan was ill-prepared for the conquest of the pre-Philippine gold islands would even be an understatement. To start with, Magellan had no more than 150 men in his three ships. These men were also unaware of Magellan's secret agenda. For that reason, they were not psychologically prepared for war with the purpose of conquest Ignorant of Magellan's secret agenda, these men had no input regarding Magellan's decisions and actions when he began the work of conquering the pre-Philippine gold islands. Magellan was practically acting alone, single-handedly doing the daunting task of conquering the gold islands, merely relying on the hope that his men would follow his orders because he was their captain-general. Simply-put, Magellan did not work with a team. His men were just taking his orders, working for him, not with him.

Another reason behind the failure of Magellan's attempt to conquer the pre-Philippine gold islands was the fact that Magellan had no knowledge and previous assessment of the capacity of the natives to resist and fight against foreign invaders. Most likely, Magellan's assessment was largely-based on the natives' physical appearance. Encountering the pre-Philippine natives for the first time, Magellan must have thought the tattoo-covered, near-naked natives were simple naïve savages who would easily surrender to intimidation and threats. What Magellan did not know was that the Vijaya natives of northeastern Mindanao and Cebu were still significantly engaged in the practice of Austronesian animistic culture and traditions. Body tattooing was an integral part of the ancient Austronesian tradition of martial arts, fighting, and warfare. If Magellan had an understanding of the deep connection between the tattoos on the bodies of the natives and the ancient Austronesian traditions of war, he would have had second thoughts about conquering the pre-Philippine gold islands on his first visit, which to his misfortune would also be his last.

If only Magellan had set aside his racism and white European superiority complex, and tried to regard the natives as fellow human beings, with their own unique culture, Magellan would have realized the extremely difficult task of a random act of conquering the pre-Philippine natives, whose civilization started from ancient pre-historic Sundaland, the Eden of the East. Perhaps if Magellan had known that the natives were descendants of Austronesians, who introduced civilization to ancient China and Mesopotamia, he might have tempered his daring aggression, and the timing of his invasion (Oppenheimer, 1998, 63-65). Then, Magellan would have avoided his untimely death.

Magellan' survivors, among them Gines de Mafra and Francisco Albo, a pilot of one of Magellan's ships, considered Magellan's death an act of foolhardy and reckless aggression. The Spanish court agreed with this opinion. (Scott, 283). It must have been in 1527 that Hernan Cortez, the Spanish viceroy in Mexico tried to send a letter of apology to the King of Cebu, probably through his cousin Alvaro de Saavedra, the captain-general of the Saavedra expedition which came from Mexico.

Although Saavedra reached Kalagan country in northeastern Mindanao, Hernan Cortez' letter of apology never reached Rajah Umabong (Humabon), the King of Cebu. It appears the hostility and resistance of the natives on the coast of Kalagan was more than enough to prevent Saavedra from sailing to Cebu.

Lapu-Lapu's Role and the Strategic Location of Mactan

A very important and critical part of the native conspiracy against Magellan was the role and participation of Datu Si Lapu-Lapu of Mactan. Contrary to the account that Si Lapu-Lapu was an enemy of the King of Cebu, and a renegade, Si Lapu-Lapu was in fact one of the main actors in the great drama of the conspiracy. Moreover, Lapu-Lapu was family. He was the uncle of Rajah Umabong's wife (Scott, 194, 283). Si Lapu-Lapu was assigned the role of renegade chief, because of the strategic location of his territory, and the designated battlefield to which Magellan would be lured.

Mactan was a deliberate choice for the battleground planned by Rajah Si Ayo and Rajah Humabon. The two kings chose not just any place, but a specific, strategic location, the northeast end of the island. The two kings figured that Magellan would attack in daylight. He needed to see the cannon artillery targets: the native warriors and their homes. At least a league out to sea, the cannon artillery from the ships could not reach the shore and would be unable to decimate the warriors and the people's homes. In order to attack Lapu-Lapu and his warriors,

Magellan and his men had to row their skiffs on the waters just above the rocks, and wade in the water before reaching the shore, where they had to fight against the native warriors in face-to-face combat. Without the artillery fire from the cannons of Magellan's ships, the native warriors would be more or less on equal footing with Magellan's men on the battlefield.

The other problem was that Magellan and his men had guns; the natives did not have any. By any measure, guns are superior to the natives' bows and arrows, spears and machetes. Considering this, Rajah Si Ayo and Rajah Humabon (Umabong) knew that the strategy to counter Magellan's superior arms and firepower was to send an overwhelming number of native warriors against his men.

While the name of Si Lapu-Lapu is mentioned several times in Pigafetta's narrative, nowhere is it indicated that Lapu-Lapu and Magellan ever had a face-to-face encounter. Even in the Battle of Mactan, it was a group of warriors who converged upon Magellan, then attacked and killed him. Lapu-Lapu was not mentioned as one of the warriors. However, this does not exclude the possibility that Lapu-Lapu was one of them.

In conclusion, the native conspiracy was tremendously successful. Despite the superior arms and firepower of Magellan's fleet, the natives were victorious, and had successfully eliminated Magellan. In fact, the native conspiracy had accomplished an amazing feat. Although an armed conflict was waged in battle, there was minimal loss of native lives, property, and infrastructure. The kingdom and Port of Cebu remained intact, even as Magellan's ships released some artillery while fleeing during the massacre of 22 survivors in the courtyard outside the palace of Rajah Humabon, who had invited them to lunch.

The three native kings of the conspiracy, the chief men of the King of Cebu, the alliance of Bisaya warriors, and the people worked together as a united force to defeat and eliminate a foreign invader using strategies drawn from their ancient

Austronesian culture and traditions. The natives effectively used diplomacy as a tool for deception, succeeding in making Magellan believe in his own lies. In the end, the natives were able to beat Magellan at his own game.

Lessons from the Success of the Native Conspiracy

Five centuries ago, the Austronesian natives of the pre-Philippines employed strategies for defense, war, and peace which remain actively applied in the world today. Faced with the surprise arrival of Ferdinand Magellan, a European invader with superior weapons of war, the natives employed indigenous defense strategies that enabled them to defeat a formidable enemy. The success of the native conspiracy and resistance against Magellan offer the following lessons:

1. Diplomacy is an excellent weapon in the first line of defense and the preservation of peace. Rajah Si Ayo, the king of Mazzaua and the Brain of the Conspiracy employed ancient Austronesian diplomatic strategies with wisdom and sophistication in dealing with Magellan's serious threats of violence and imminent invasion. Rajah Si Ayo's diplomatic maneuvers effectively delayed a direct frontal war with Magellan giving the natives time to gather a large fighting force, and prepare a smart action plan against Magellan.

2. The game of deception can be played by all competing parties involved in a conflict. The pre-Philippine natives played their part so well in the game of deception that Magellan initiated. In fact, they were able to make Magellan believe in his own lies and beat him at his own game. In a game of fools it is naïve and foolhardy to assume that any one party has the monopoly and control of the bag of tricks.

3. Superior weapons are not a guarantee for victory in war. In the Battle of Mactan, the firepower of the large artillery from the cannons of Magellan's galleons were rendered useless. The natives had lured Magellan to a strategic battle ground in Mactan Island, a place far enough from the reach of the artillery from Magellan's ships. The rocky shores of the north end of Mactan prevented Magellan's ships from getting enough proximity to the shore resulting in the failure of the artillery from Magellan's ships to decimate the native warriors and the natives' homes near the shore.

4. Engaging the enemy in a proxy battle ground preserves the integrity of the socio-economic and political infrastructure of a society and saves the lives of its people. The natives engaged the enemy in proxy war location, a strategy used by today's military superpowers. They lured Magellan to a battle ground away from the socio-economic and population center. Diverting the war to Mactan Island saved the international port of the capital city, the seat of power of the kingdom of Cebu, and above all, the lives of its people from destruction.

5. Unity is strength. A people united against an invader or a common enemy has a greater chance at success and victory in war. Moreover, the natives who were bound together by a common Bisaya cultural identity proved to be a formidable force. Their indigenous Austronesian Vizzaya (Bisaya) culture and traditions in the Vizzaya islands and northern Mindanao brought the natives together as one people, and gave them the wisdom and strength to defend their native land with the will to resist, fight, and defeat Magellan, a foreign invader.

REFERENCES

1.   Antonio Pigafetta, Magellan's Voyage: A Narrative Account of the First Circumnavigation, Translated and Edit ed by R.A. Skelton, New York, Dover Publications, Inc. Copyright Yale University, (1969) pp. 42, 43-53, 64 -69, 70 -75, 88 -89, 94-95.

2.   William Henry Scott, Barangay. Ateneo de Manila University Press, (1994) pp. 1, 2, 4, 6, 7, 9, 32, 63, 128, 129, 143, 161 -162, 164 -165, 194, 220, 274, 276, 283.

3.   Margarita Cembrano, Patterns of the Past: The Ethno Archaeology of Butuan. A Publication of the Museum of the Philippines, (September 1998) pp. 19, 21, 24, 25, 26, 27, 28, 29.

4.   Greg Hontiveros, Butuan of a Thousand Years, Published by the Butuan City Historical & Cultural Foundation, Inc. (2004) pp. 16, 24, 25, 26, 27, 78, 82-86, 89, 103 -104, 127, 149, 176.

5.   Greg Hontiveros, A Fire on the Island, A Fresh Look at the First Mass Controversy. Published by the Butuan City Historical and Cultural Foundation, Inc. (2008) pp. 22-25.

6.   Gabriel B. Atega, 2007. Mazzawa and The Celebrations of the First Philippine Holy Week. Midtown printing Co. Inc. Book Development and Publishing Division, Davao City, Philippines, (2007) pp. 118-119.

REFERENCES

7.   Gabriel B. Atega, Where is Mazzawa? Sweet Tree Inc. Da vao City, Philippines (2010) p. 9.

8.   Stephen Oppenheimer, 1998. Eden in the East: The Drowned Continent of Southeast Asia. Orion Publishing Group Ltd. London, U.K. (1998) pp. 50, 63-65, 78.

9.   Ramon N. Villegas, Kayamanan, the Philippine Jewelry Tradition. Central Bank of the Philippines, Manila, (1983).

10. Ramon N. Villegas, GINTO History Wrought in Gold. Bangko Central ng Pilipinas, (2004) pp. 80, 169, 182-189.

11. Lane Wilcken, 2010. Filipino Tattoos Ancient to Modern, Schiffer Publishing Ltd. Atglen Pennsylvania, U.S.A. 2010.

12. Gregorio F. Zaide & Sonia M. Zaide, Philippine History and Government, All Nations Publishing Co. Inc. (2002) p. 59.

13. Paul Lunde, The Explorer Marco Polo. Saudi Aramco World, (July – August 2005) Volume 56, Number 4.

14. D. Cyranoski. 2009. Nature International Weekly Journal of Science, Dec. 2009.

15. Hannibal Carado. Spanish Expeditions to the Philippines, (SCRIBD).

REFERENCES

16.   Jesus Peralta. 2011. The Austronesian Expansion – A Re action to Paths of Origin Manila, Philippines, National Commission for Culture and the Arts, June 14, 2011.

17.   Caraga Watch. October 2009.

18.   Encyclopedia Britannica. eb.com.

19.   MSN Encarta, Kingdom of Sri Vijaya.

20.   WikiPilipinas, Austronesian Migration Theory.

21.   Wikipedia, Ferdinand Magellan: Aftermath and Legacy.

22.   Wikipedia, The Malay Race.

23.   Wikipedia, Rajahnate of Cebu.

24.   Wikipedia, Rajah Humabon.

25.   Wikipedia, Guiuan Airfield, (July 2018) pp. 1, 2.

26.   Wikipedia, Guiuan Airport, (August 15, 2017) p. 1.

27.   Wikipedia, Garcia Jofre de Loaisa.

REFERENCES

28. Wikipedia, The Saavedra Expedition.

29. Wikipedia, Lopez de Villalobos Expedition.

30. Wikipedia, Ruy Lopez de Villalobos.

31. Wikipedia, Sarangani.

32. The Biography, https://thebiography.us.

33. Historical Background of Caraga.
    http://caraga.denr.gov.ph.

34. Butuan Archaelogical sites, UNESCO World Heritage
    Centre, http:// whc. Unesco.org/en/tentativelists/2071.

35. Moonsoon Winds to the "Land of Gold", http://
    orlas.berkeley.edu/spice/textobjects/overview.htm.

36. Gold of Ancestors, Pre-colonial Treasures in the Philip-
    pines, http://www.ayalamuseum.org.

37. Enrique of Melaka, The Age of Discovery.
    http://www.sabrizain.org/malay/port3.htm.

REFERENCES

38.   James C. Montgomery, USN and Franklin B. Montgomery, USAF, Guiuan, Samar, The Philippines,

http://www.Seabees93.net/MEM-SAMAR-index.htm.

CPSIA information can be obtained
at www.ICGtesting.com
Printed in the USA
FSHW020118300921
85105FS

9 781733 677905